SHAMBHALA DRAGON EDITIONS

The dragon is an age-old symbol of the highest spiritual essence,
embodying wisdom, strength, and the divine power of
transformation. In this spirit, Shambhala Dragon Editions offers a
treasury of readings in the sacred knowledge of Asia. In presenting
the works of authors both ancient and modern, we seek to make
these teachings accessible to lovers of wisdom everywhere.
Each Shambhala Dragon Edition features Smyth-sewn binding and is
printed on acid-free paper.

Bodhisattva of Compassion

The Mystical Tradition of Kuan Yin

John Blofeld

SHAMBHALA
Boston
1988

SHAMBHALA PUBLICATIONS, INC.
HORTICULTURAL HALL
300 MASSACHUSETTS AVENUE
BOSTON, MASSACHUSETTS 02115

© 1977 by John Blofeld

9 8 7 6 5 4 3 2

Printed in the United States of America

Distributed in the United States by Random House and in Canada by Random House of Canada Ltd.

Library of Congress Cataloging-in-Publication Data
Blofeld, John Eaton Calthorpe, 1913–1987.
    Bodhisattva of compassion: the mystical tradition of Kuan Yin / John Blofeld.
        p.   cm. — (Shambhala dragon editions)
    ISBN 0-87773-126-8 (pbk.)
    1. Avalokiteśvara (Buddhist deity) I. Title.
BQ4710.A8B57 1988
294.3′4211—dc19   87-28524
                CIP

To Suwimol, my daughter and Kuan Yin's devotee

Contents

Illustrations

Acknowledgements

My warmest thanks are due to several people who went to great trouble to supply me with valuable materials in English and Chinese and with illustrations, especially the Venerable Hsüan Hua and his disciples at Gold Mountain Monastery, San Francisco; and my good friends Shojun Bando, Hirofumi Ando (translator of the four little Japanese pilgrim songs), Gerald Yorke, David Kidd and Gary Thomson. I am very grateful, also, to the British Museum authorities and to Major W. H. Edmonds for allowing me to reproduce photographs of paintings and statues in their collections. Finally, I acknowledge my debt to those two outstanding reference works, Getty's *Gods of Northern Buddhism* and Edmunds' *Pointers and Clues to Subjects in Chinese and Japanese Art.*

Foreword

Radiance, spotless and effulgent,
Night-dispelling Sun of Wisdom!
                    Lotus Sūtra

This is in part the story of a quest, of gradual progress towards the heart of an enigma. Confronted some forty years ago by the charming figure of Kuan Yin, known to many as the Chinese Goddess of Love, I came to wonder whether it was wholly symbolic or whether Kuan Yin could, in some sense, be said to *be*. The adventure started one night when, by the uncertain light of votive candles, I had made my way alone through the shadows to the back of a temple hall. The fitful gleams playing amidst the darkness conjured up an atmosphere of mystery. As I stood gazing up at a tall bronze statue of Kuan Yin, a door seemed to open in my mind and the goddess, so I could have sworn, *deigned to address me!* Imagination? That may well seem to have been so, but who under such romantic circumstances could resist the hope that she had really spoken? Thenceforth I was her devoted follower, which does not mean, however, that I quite believed in her. Drawn by a fascination having nothing to do with belief or its converse, I delved ever more deeply beyond the guise she wears for simple folk and presently came to have some dim apprehension of her significance as a celestial Bodhisattva, a kind of beingless being representing one of the most exalted concepts of Mahayana Buddhism. Perceiving her to be much more than a graceful myth expressing the yearning of the poor and lonely for compassion, I had all the more reason for loving her; yet this new vision of her as the embodiment of divine love was somewhat marred by the miraculous powers attributed to her in the sutras. The passages describing them seemed at first to detract from rather than enhance her sublimity, for they struck me as too fanciful and more becoming to a folk goddess than a celestial Bodhisattva. This, of course, was just a personal view.

Years later, with an insight stemming from the teaching of my Chinese and Tibetan masters, I came to understand what I still think is her true significance – or part of it. *She is real* – oh, not as Artemis and Aphrodite were real in the eyes of their worshippers, but in a sense more secret and profound. However, in trying to make this point, I have not sought to convert others to my way of thinking. I shall be happy if they come to love her, even if she remains for them just a beautiful idea. To give colour and life to my portrait of her, I have related many Chinese and Tibetan tales which reveal her at what may rightly or wrongly be called the lower and middle levels of understanding, besides setting down some of her mantras and appropriate excerpts from sutras and manuals of contemplative meditation. Also I have had much to say of Kuan Yin's three progenitors – Avalokiteśvara (Chenresigs) and Tara, two deities warmly cherished by Tibetans, and the Chinese Princess Miao Shan, for Kuan Yin is mysteriously all of these together!

Perhaps the portrait will find favour not only with some who are interested in Buddhism and Chinese and Tibetan yogic practice, but also with those who have come upon temples and shrines to Kuan Yin while sojourning in Asian countries, and with the many lovers of Chinese art who have fallen captive to her charms both as a benign mother goddess and as a sweetly smiling maiden deity. I should have liked to say more of her from the viewpoint of Chinese and Japanese art, but research facilities in Bangkok are limited. As it is, the pith of what I have written is mystical rather than aesthetic; I hope it may encourage those who, without necessarily subscribing to an established faith, have glimpsed the effulgence of what Lao-tzû called the Nameless – that which once inspired certain Greeks to erect a wayside altar to 'The Unknown God' and led Wordsworth to perceive a supernatural radiance suffusing the world around him. The Nameless is as it is and quite beyond the realm of conceptual thought; yet there are times when one needs to hint at it symbolically. To my mind, Kuan Yin's gentle form is a worthier symbol than the figure of a tortured being hanging from a cross or of an awesome father god. Trivial and inaccurate as all such symbols are in comparison with the reality they clothe, they have their importance and should be chosen with care. If we are to preserve our sanity amidst the mind-shattering

horrors of the modern world, it is well to have an intimation
of serenely abiding beauty underlying the grim façade visible
to our senses. Could we but *choose* our own symbol of that
beauty (and why indeed should we not?), it would be hard to
find a form lovelier than Kuan Yin's; or, if the Chinese conception of the goddess seems just a trifle too sedate, we could
opt for her Tibetan counterpart and twin, the compassionate
and slyly playful Tara!

JOHN BLOFELD

Bodhisattva
of Compassion

Chapter 1

The Enigma

No lover of fair visions
Born of mind and caught
By the painter's brush
Or carver's hand
Can well resist
Kuan Yin's enchantment.

No follower of the Way
Beyond the Hidden Gate
But longs to read the secret
Reflected in her eyes,
To know what lies behind
Her enigmatic smile.

Whence rose that shining being,
Divine embodiment
Of pure compassion?
Whence came such faith
In Kuan Yin's power
To ferry sentient beings
Across samsara's ocean?

Where did she first appear
And how acquire
Her mellifluous name
– Kuan Shih Yin,
Hearer-of-Cries?

Among these questions, the last is soonest answered. Kuan Yin (or Kuan Shih Yin, to give the name its proper form) means She-Who-Hearkens-to-the-Cries-of-the-World, and is a translation of the Sanskrit name of her chief progenitor, Avalokiteśvara (or Avalokita). In Korea and Japan and, above all, in China before the Red flood engulfed her temples there, Kuan Yin has been popularly revered as a goddess for a thousand years or more, though in truth she is not a goddess but a celestial Bodhisattva and was formerly embodied in male form, as is sometimes the case to this day. By the learned it is known that she is not to be found among the deities of mountains, groves and streams, or to be numbered among the high divinities of heaven. That she has long been venerated as a goddess by all kinds of people, ranging from fisher-folk to Taoist sages in their mountain hermitages, as well as by Buddhist laymen generally, is because of the irresistible appeal made by so compassionate a deity to a race intimately acquainted with poverty and oppression throughout its long history.

Until recently, shrines to Kuan Yin stood in all kinds of places throughout the length and breadth of China and in several neighbouring countries as well; wherever possible, these shrines were placed near running water or overlooking a lake or sea, and she is often depicted by painters as seated on a rock gazing out across the water, or standing upon a floating lotus petal. Her dwelling stands on a sea-girt island and many fisher-folk and boat-people have come to identify her with their own patron goddess, so that each deity is sometimes credited with characteristics of the other. I think it best to introduce her as a goddess of fishermen, for that is the guise in which I myself first saw her in a temple of her own.

Often during a journey in South China, having halted at a townlet about an hour before sunset and arranged for a night's lodging at an inn, if I strolled beside a river or along the seashore I would come to some pleasant spot in the outskirts where stood a temple to Kuan Yin. Set amidst clumps of trees or near the top of some rocky crag would be a gateway where, suspended beneath the curving eaves, would hang a lacquered board inscribed in gold calligraphy with characters bearing some allusion to her name. Beyond would lie a courtyard, so narrow in some cases as to be called a 'sky-well' and then a fantastically roofed temple with walls of grey brick and doors of lacquered wood. The first time this happened, the temple proved to be scarcely more than a shrine-room about the size of the chapel in some modest old Catholic house in England, or smaller. The goddess was represented by a crumbling plaster statue from which the colours had long faded. A clumsily built table daubed with flaking scarlet lacquer did duty as an altar. The place, though redolent of poverty, had an air of being much frequented. I had barely had time to take in the ancient beams, the faded calligraphic inscriptions, tattered banners and coarse china furnishings of the altar when I heard the sound of many footsteps in the courtyard. Not wishing to be in the way, I would have left, had not the caretaker, an old man clad in shabby trousers of black cotton and a singlet grey with long use, given me an understanding smile and gestured for me to stay.

A group of boat-women came hurrying in. Dressed in pyjama-suits of cheap, black cloth, some had broad-brimmed bamboo hats strapped to their backs, while others carried their babies there comfortably seated in cocoons of crimson cloth tied to their mothers' jackets, legs wide apart and dangling. Glancing somewhat askance at the tall foreign devil from the Western Ocean, they sank to their knees and kowtowed three times with a grace I had not expected from people of such coarse appearance ('coarse' is perhaps too strong a word to be apt for Chinese peasants, but they certainly looked like people who led hard lives). Soon they rose from their knees, except for one young girl in an advanced state of pregnancy who remained with her face to the floor-cushion. Lighting incense-sticks and candles taken from a table near the door, they chanted a brief and far from tuneful melody, then repeated their kowtows and hurried away led by the pregnant girl. The whole performance took perhaps three or four minutes.

'What was that about?' I asked the caretaker in my still rudimentary Chinese, though I scarcely needed to be told.

'The young one has happiness in her. Did you not see? The others are her relatives. They came to pray that the child will be á boy.'

'And she will surely get a son?' I said, smiling.

'Kuan Yin is kind.'

'I see. And what must the mother do to earn Kuan Yin's favour?'

'Do? When her son is born, she will come to give thanks.'

It was as simple as that. Later, a Chinese friend explained that it was not customary for suppliants to bargain with the goddess. No need for the mother to promise to be good or undertake that her son would requite the favour in any way. Kuan Yin, being compassionate, would naturally be happy to grant such a wish. 'But suppose the girl has a daughter?' I insisted.

'Then the girl-baby will be destined to a singularly fortunate existence. The goddess would not deny so harmless a request without good reason.'

Perhaps my friend was being ironical, but what he said certainly accorded with what the boat-women believed. The peasants' conception of Kuan Yin was uncomplicated. She could be relied upon to behave like a fondly indulgent parent, provided only that one's wish was not evil in itself. No special degree of piety or strict conduct was required of the petitioners beyond firm belief in Kuan Yin's power to aid. Such fairy god-mothers, I reflected sadly, can surely not exist outside story books; but it was nice to think of the joy and comfort fisher-folk and farmers derived from their simple belief. As a prep-school kid of eleven or so, fear that God would get back at me by some such means as ensuring that my school report would be bad enough to anger my father had made me a good deal more virtuous than I was by nature, causing me to tell the truth at highly inconvenient moments and be sure to empty my bowels *every* day lest the affirmative ticks I pencilled in a certain book should not reflect my actual performance. I was glad to know that Kuan Yin was much less exacting.

To my everlasting regret, I did not while in China visit P'u T'o Shan (or P'u-t'o-lo-k'a Mountain), an island off the Che-kiang coast which takes its name from the Sanskrit word Potala, meaning Kuan Yin's Paradise. For that is the holiest place in the world to devotees of the goddess. One of the stories relating to it tells of an Indian ascetic who, arriving there during the T'ang Dynasty, entered the sacred Ch'ao-Yin Cave (Cave-where-the-Voice-of-the-Tide-is-Heard) and burnt off all his fingers as an offering to Kuan Yin! How singularly inappropri-ate! Of all the deities of this universe, there is none so averse to burnt offerings as the Goddess of Mercy. It is pleasanter to accept another popular account of the island's earliest claim to sanctity, from which we learn that Kuan Yin visited it in person – an event of which picturesque evidence remains in the form of her footprint embedded in the rock called Kuan Yin's Leap, its depth being due to the momentum of her jump from the neighbouring island of Lo Chia Shan.

In another sense, of course, Kuan Yin permanently inhabits P'u T'o Island (unless she has recently left it to avoid being sub-jected to the thoughts of Mao Tse-tung). There are innumer-able stories of her having manifested herself to pilgrims, usually in the Ch'ao-Yin Cave; at such times, however, she remains invisible to any of her visitors who have seriously transgressed against the dictates of compassion. At high tide the cave is filled with waters so turbulent that, from time to time, a geyser twenty feet high spouts from a hole in the roof; so pilgrims have to wait until the tide is low if they desire to be received in audience. It is said that the compassionate among them behold the sands mysteriously transformed into a carpet of white lotus, whence a pink lotus of enormous size arises to form a throne for the goddess. It is easy to be scornful of such stories, but I am sure the atmosphere in the cave has a haunting quality which disposes one to expect every kind of marvel. I know from my own experiences in similar places how easily normal scepticism becomes suspended. That Kuan Yin is actually seen with the eyes in one's head I doubt, but with the inner eye? Some who claim to have had this vision are people whose truthfulness is beyond question. If one feels compelled to doubt them, the most that can be said is that pilgrims keyed up by high expectation and worked upon by the place's curiously eerie atmosphere may have thought they perceived what they ardently desired to see. Personally I think there was rather more to it than that, but there is a whole range of experience that would be difficult to classify as purely objective or subjective, so each of us has to interpret such phenomena in the way that seems best to him.

I was to live in China for some time before coming to understand correctly what my more learned Buddhist friends meant by insisting that Kuan Yin is not a goddess but a celestial Bodhisattva. This was first explained to me by a Mr P'an, who knew something of Sanskrit and was quite an authority on Chinese Buddhism. One day, hearing me refer to Kuan Yin as a goddess, he said reprovingly: 'Don't speak of Kuan Yin like that, Ah Jon. You sound as though you supposed that, if they happen to be Buddhists, even scholars – "book-perfume men" as we call them – share the simple beliefs you find among peasants.'

Having but the vaguest idea of his meaning, I answered, smiling: 'I shall be delighted to call her a celestial Bodhisattva, but isn't that just another name for what might irreverently be called a super-goddess, that is someone nearer the top of the celestial hierarchy? I really don't see that it makes much difference.'

He could not help laughing; but, presently, speaking seriously, he went on to give me a metaphysical explanation that took some grasping. His English, though very good indeed, was not quite up to the task and, at one stage, he ran upstairs for a dictionary. That proved to be scarcely any help at all to someone trying to render from one language to another the terminology of Mahayana Buddhism. Here I have set down his discourse (with the help of a fair degree of hind-knowledge) not as it was given, but as I think he intended to give it.

'You must realise first of all that our minds are not separate from Mind, which, if you have read any Ch'an (Zen) works, you will know to be the sole reality. Known in its quiescent state as the Great Void or what you English people call Ultimate Reality, it is *simultaneously* the realm of form, "the matrix of the myriad objects", as Lao-Tzû puts it. By no means must they be thought of as separate. The Great Void and the realm of form *are not two!* There is no going from the one to the other, only a transmutation of your mode of perception. Mind is like a boundless ocean of light, or infinite space, from which streams forth Bodhi, a marvellous energy that produces in us an urge towards Enlightenment. But to attain Enlightenment, you need vast stores of wisdom and compassion in perfect union. Wisdom includes full and direct perception of your own egolessness and of the non-existence of anything like "own-self" in any object. Compassion is the prime means of destroying all clinging to delusory selfhood. From Bodhi emanate particularised streams of liberating energy – the energies of wisdom, compassion, of the pure activity needed to combine them, and so forth. These, in turn, subdivide and thus become more tangible to minds deluded by the false notion of self-existing egos and self-existing objects. In some marvellous way, these streams and substreams become embodied in forms like those which divinities are thought to have, the primary streams as what we call celestial Buddhas, the secondary streams as what are called celestial Bodhisattvas.

'Amitābha Buddha embodies the primary liberating energy of compassion; Avalokita Bodhisattva embodies its secondary emanation. This doctrine is derived from a yogic tradition taught at Nalanda University in India almost two millenia ago. As to Kuan Yin, our peculiarly Chinese embodiment of compassion, she was originally identical with Avalokita and therefore visualised as possessing male characteristics. Some people suppose that the change in sex attributed to the Bodhisattva occurred only after a legendary Chinese princess called Miao Shan became integrated with that being through the powerful influence of our native folklore. That is certainly nonsense. Educated people do not seriously accept the Miao Shan legends. Besides, you can hardly suppose that we Chinese Buddhists, after scrupulously preserving the doctrines, practices and symbols carried back from India by monks who had made fearful journeys through burning deserts and icy mountain wastes, would have permitted such a change in sex to come about through mere *carelessness*! The key to the mystery was taught me by my teacher's teacher during a visit to Mongolia. There he came across images of Tara whom Mongols and Tibetans revere as a female emanation of Avalokita. Later on, my teacher, who loved to view collections of antique paintings, came upon several very old ones in which Kuan Yin was portrayed as being almost identical with Tara. In other words, for whatever reason, we Chinese decided to combine Avalokita and Tara into a sort of female Avalokita, whom we call Kuan Yin.'

Well, whether or not Mr P'an was exactly right about the origin of Kuan Yin's portrayal in female form, the Bodhisattva is far from being a figure of poetic whimsy. Yogically she corresponds to an actual energy permanently latent in the mind; though it may be that the *forms* in which she is envisaged are deliberate human creations. Still, I think that the artists who have best succeeded in capturing the magic of those forms must have beheld them in their meditations, for only in the stillness of one-pointed contemplation is such perfection often revealed. The 'reality' of the Bodhisattva is not hard to accept, once one recognises that even such solid-seeming objects as elephants and mountains are all creations of Mind and therefore on a par with dreams, imaginings, visions – like everything else in existence. A mental image of Kuan Yin does not differ in an ultimate sense from the floor and ceiling of the room where one sits meditating. This is a mystic's view, but one that may come to be widely accepted now that both philosophers and physicists are veering in the direction of believing that the whole universe is a mental creation.

This brief explanation of the nature of celestial Bodhisattvas may, alas, be far from lucid. In dealing with what pertains to mystical perception, explanations are seldom satisfactory, so greatly do words distort and diminish the reality they are used to convey. We may, for the moment, put aside the question of

Kuan Yin's reality; the sheer beauty of the concept of an exquisitely lovely being whose chief attribute is pure, unwavering compassion is in itself appealing enough to claim our admiration. Even when brought down to the level of a goddess – and it is thus that painters and sculptors often portray her – Kuan Yin is unique among the heavenly hierarchy in being utterly free from pride or vengefulness and reluctant to punish even those to whom a severe lesson would be salutary. The cursing of the withered fig-tree and the whipping of the temple money-changers which so disfigure the otherwise beautiful gospel stories are without counterparts among the exploits attributed to Kuan Yin.

Chapter 2

Some Manifestations

To hear her name and see her form
Delivers beings from every woe.
                              Lotus Sūtra

The embassy of the boat-women to Kuan Yin's temple well
exemplifies how peasants in China and neighbouring countries
conceive of her. Seeing her as a benevolent goddess into whose
nature it would be discourteous to enquire, they rejoice because
she is lovely in herself and generous in heeding supplications.
This uncomplicated attitude is not limited to illiterate followers
of ancient folk-religions, for even among the general run of
Buddhists in China and Japan, the distinction between deities
and celestial Bodhisattvas is blurred. However, more erudite
Buddhists see her otherwise. The following account of an experience significant to me personally prefaces two other stories
that will serve as a preview of some of the ways in which Kuan
Yin is conceptualised. One, though it does just touch upon
the Mind Only doctrine lying at the root of the celestial Bodhisattva concept, reveals her in a guise very similar to that of a
goddess, whereas the other carries us to a high metaphysical
level.

   One of the three main annual festivals of Kuan Yin, Hearer-
of-Cries, falls on the nineteenth day of the sixth lunar month
(about July). For centuries it has been celebrated by gatherings
in her honour, some of which assemble on the twelfth of the
month and spend no less than seven days on rites and contemplative meditation centred on Kuan Yin. Alas, in recent years
the ranks of her followers have been thinned. For all I know,

such festivals still take place in Japan, Korea and Singapore, but hardly in China or Viet-Nam.

Quite soon after my arrival in China, while staying at a monastery nestling among clumps of lychee-trees on the sunny side of a minor sacred mountain, I heard that 'Kuan Yin's Birthday' was going to be celebrated that evening at a neighbouring temple over which she presided, so at sunset I set off in that direction. By the time I arrived, night had fallen. Scudding clouds obscured the moon, but peach-shaped lanterns suspended from the temple gateway's elegantly curving roof cast a pool of crimson light that could be seen from a distance. Beyond lay a courtyard thronged with worshippers whose faces were illumined by the rays of perhaps a hundred candles streaming through the shrine-hall's wide-flung doors. Most were lay-people, but a sprinkling of bald pates showed that some monks and nuns from neighbouring monasteries were among them. All were craning their heads towards the shrine where Kuan Yin's statue rose behind a lavishly carved and gilded altar where stood innumerable candle-sticks, a great bronze incense tripod and an array of porcelain vessels piled with offerings of fruit and flowers. No animal flesh or cups of wine were to be seen, for even the peasants had some inkling of the difference between Kuan Yin and the more gluttonous local deities; besides, the keepers of the shrine would have rejected such offerings as impure and displeasing to the Bodhisattva – though not monks, they would hardly have accepted them even for themselves.

The night air, drenched with the mingled perfumes of burning sandalwood and of jasmine and champak flowers, quivered as the mallet thudded upon a large hollowed block known as the wooden-fish drum; its throb was punctuated by the clang and tinkle of bronze and silver instruments used to mark the rhythm of the chant. Though the same few words, *Namu ta-tzû ta-pei Kuan Shih Yin P'u-Sa* (Homage to the greatly compassionate, greatly merciful Kuan Shih Yin Bodhisattva)! were intoned repeatedly, the ardour of those taking part and frequent subtle changes in the rhythm dispelled monotony, so that the music lifted me into a realm of beauty and enchantment.

Taller than the wiry southerners pressing all about me, I had an unobstructed view. The Bodhisattva was depicted as a gracious young lady with smoothly rounded cheeks and chin, sitting very informally upon a rock-like throne, one knee raised so high that the elegant little slipper peeping from beneath her robe was on a level with the other knee. One slender hand toyed with a willow sprig, the other held a vase of 'sweet dew' symbolising the nectar of compassion. To either side, wrought on a smaller scale, stood her attendants – Shan Ts'ai, a smiling boy, and Lung Nü, the Dragon Maiden, who was holding out a giant pearl. These statues can hardly have been the work of local artists; they were finely sculpted and had a pleasing liveliness, though I could have wished them less ornate. But for her distinctive posture and the nature of the symbols in her hands, the splendidly robed and bejewelled figure could almost have been mistaken for that of Mary arrayed as Queen of Heaven in the manner of South Europe. Superficially at least, her robes and ornaments resembled artifacts from Byzantium. Struck by this lavish costume, I wondered how this empress-like being could be made to fit in with the gently austere teaching of the Buddha; for I had still to learn that the external forms taken by Buddhism in different countries, though strikingly varied, entail no real departures from its doctrines.

Presently a gust of wind sent incense-smoke billowing upwards in heavy clouds that momentarily blurred the Bodhisattva's features, creating the illusion of a living being whose expression now altered and took on unimaginable beauty. As though chiding my churlishness in the matter of her costume, she seemed to fix me with her eyes and gently shake her head.

Aware that this was no miracle, I was nevertheless entranced and tried hard to believe that the goddess had taken notice of me. What is more, there seemed to hover just beyond the threshold of my mind a teasing recollection of something or someone once greatly loved but long faded from my memory. The effect was so poignant that I wanted both to laugh and to cry. I am convinced that it was this elusive recollection rather than the trick wrought by the incense smoke that produced what seems in retrospect a magical effect; in that moment I conceived a reverence for the Compassionate One which, far from fading with the years, was destined to intensify, although for a long time it remained no more than a pleasant whimsy. In those days

I had not the wisdom to reconcile deep devotion to a deity with the knowledge that deities are not!

I was too moved to pay attention to what followed. No doubt the long period of invocation gave place to recitation of the P'u Mên chapter of the Lotus Sūtra or of Kuan Yin's Dhāranī of Great Compassion. The rite must have ended with an inspiring crescendo of cymbals and drums succeeded by an eerie silence as the officiants prostrated themselves; but by then I had slipped away to begin my walk through the darkness to the monastery where I lodged. To this day I recall my pleasure in the cool night air so free from cloying scents, the creek of bamboos swaying in the wind and the scurrying of small creatures in the undergrowth. Throughout the walk I indulged the poetic fancy that the goddess had wished to remind me of something immensely important to my happiness. Such a mood is not difficult to sustain while strolling by moonlight on the slopes of a mountain where immortal beings have been worshipped since before the dawn of history; the very atmosphere is vibrant with intimations of their presence. To a part of my mind which told me I was being absurd, I put up strenuous resistance, being loath to return to an ugly world which, even in those days, was fast coming under the domination of monsters disguised as inventors and technicians. Having disposed of cavilling logic, my mind soared, leading me to a state bordering on ecstasy. I had a foretaste of the wisdom born of full realisation that only mind is real; the demons of duality were temporarily vanquished so that it became possible to entertain simultaneously two opposing facets of truth.

Back at the monastery, while waiting for the sleepy porter to admit me, I became aware of a delicious fragrance which I supposed to have a supernatural origin until, looking up, I saw that the gateway was overhung by the boughs of a tree called in Chinese *yeh-lai-hsiang* (night fragrance) which pours out its perfume during the first watches of the night. The great courtyard was in darkness, the monks being still away celebrating the festival or else retired to their cells to sleep or meditate until summoned for the morning rite an hour before dawn. Noticing that lamps still glimmered in the deserted shrine-hall, I felt a sudden impulse to enter and make my way round behind the Buddha statues to where it was customary in Chinese monasteries to house a statue of Kuan Yin. There she was, standing upon a shelf at about the level of my chest. It was an image of fine bronze some three feet high, with the right hand raised in benediction, the elongated eyes half closed in contemplative bliss. The stumps of votive candles still guttered at her feet, whereas the incense sticks lit in her honour had burnt down to the stubs leaving behind a sour staleness. It seems sad that deities have to endure this odour when their worshippers have retired for the night. Perhaps the truth is that it is the worshippers themselves who enjoy temple offerings. Lighting fresh incense, I stood before her in silence until, suddenly carried away by exaltation, I whispered: 'Compassionate One, be pleased to speak and convince me of your reality'!

How foolish this must sound and how ashamed I should be to write of it, were it not for the sequel. Even with the words upon my lips I reflected that a sane man should know better than to attempt holding converse with a statue! Yet perhaps I had some excuse; for, apart from being then in a special state of mind, I had recently spent much time in the company of certain Chinese Buddhists who, despite being men of obvious good sense and erudition, would have found nothing surprising in such conduct. As it turned out, no justification was needed, for the plain truth is that the statue answered me at once, saying: 'Look not for my reality in the realm of appearances or in the Void. Seek it in your own mind. There only it resides.'

I wish I could make the story even more extraordinary by affirming that the bronze lips moved, that the beautifully moulded throat gave forth melodious sounds. It was not so. No sound or movement stirred the silence. The enigmatic words entered my consciousness as thought-forms, but so palpably that not even sound itself could have made the effect more electrifying or their sequence more precise. It is hard to believe that, at a time when my knowledge of Mahayana Buddhism was so slight, I could have summoned such a pronouncement from within myself. I did not really know then what the first sentence meant. I felt sure I had received an intimation that Kuan Yin exists – to the extent that 'exists' is a fitting description of her subtle nature. Using the word thus is perhaps to overstate the case, just as to say that she does not exist would be to understate it. My experience was not imaginary. Such intuitive perceptions

are too direct, too penetrating to be mistaken for ordinary imaginings. Yet for years I hesitated to speak of it, except to my
Chinese friends, who understood its nature; but now I have
come to recognise that no good purpose is served by concealing
marvels merely because people nowadays are apt to disbelieve
them. In truth, such a marvel is not magical to those who
recognise mind's sovereign power over phenomena of every
kind whatsoever.

> Chrysanthemums *are* gold
> To those who see them so.
> Red gold is just a metal
> Till thought-forms give it worth.

There is a modern short story about a timid knight who,
armed with a magic word to make him invulnerable, slew fifty
dragons as easily as cockroaches. Unfortunately, while engaged
in slaying the fiftieth, he suddenly realised that he had been
tricked by his teacher into putting faith in a made-up nonsense-
word. Needless to say, his fifty-first dragon gobbled him up in
no time at all! Yet can one say that the magic wrought by his
faith in that nonsense-word was not real? It stood him in far
better stead than his 'real' armour and 'objectively existing'
sword!

A British-educated Chinese friend of mine once told me a
story that fully bears out this view of reality.

'As you know, though my mother was a Buddhist, I received
all my pre-university education at Catholic schools, was bap-
tised at sixteen and later took a Catholic wife. For years I was
as devout a convert as could reasonably be expected of a man
like me, a geologist. Then came the war which sent so many
of us fleeing westward before the Japanese advance. My native
city suffered cruelly from indiscriminate rape and slaughter. I
could not think of my old home without tears. My work for
a government prospecting enterprise took me to some wild and
lonely places in Kweichow province and once I was sent to look
for wolfram in a mountainous region six or seven days walk from
the nearest motor-road. One day, an hour before our usual stop
for midday rice, I mistook a mule-track for the path we were
following and wandered far away from the men carrying my

luggage and equipment. Knowing I was lost, but hungry and convinced by occasional fresh piles of mule dung that the track must lead to human habitations, I pressed forward. Upward and upward I went until clouds were swirling about me and I could hear what sounded like the weird cries of gibbons high up in the trees. At every turn I hoped in vain to come upon at least a woodsman's hovel, but I had wandered too far by then to feel it wise to turn back. I needed food and some local man to guide me to where my porters were likely to be found.

'An icy wind came tearing down from the high peaks and dusk was closing in. Eerie sounds were all about me, some recognisable as the voices of wind and stream, others inexplicable and mournful as the cries of wandering ghosts. With each step I grew more afraid and the mists swirling among the rocks grew denser and more opaque. Fears of wild beasts rose to haunt me; as for bandits, of whom the local people had told me sinister tales, I longed to meet a fellow-human being, bandit or not. At last terror brought me to my knees beside the path and, teeth chattering, I poured out a prayer to my patron saint, St Bernadette, begging that sweet child (as I thought of her) to appear and lead me to a place of safety. By what light remained, my eyes sought for her among the rocks. I believed that if she did not come, I should lose my sanity, if not my life!

'Then she was there, standing on a small flat rock, her flimsy blue robe hardly ruffled by the fierce and bitterly cold wind. She was smiling, as I could see well, for around her glowed a nimbus of soft light. Gradually I took in that there was something unexpected about her face. Then I realised what it was – she was a *Chinese* Bernadette! Her high-swept hair, the jewelled ornaments clasped about her throat, the white silk trousers peeping through a blue robe slit to the thigh were those of a noble Chinese maiden many centuries ago.

' "Come, Elder Brother," she said, speaking melodious Mandarin in a childish voice too young to have belonged to Bernadette even at the time of her first meeting with the Holy Virgin, "I shall show you a place where you can rest safely and tomorrow all will be very well."

'She led me a short distance to a shallow cave well protected from the wind. Its floor was as soft as the softest of beds and

I am nearly sure I caught sight of a silken *pei-wo* (quilt) stuffed no doubt with warm silk-floss, just as I fell asleep in the very act of lying down at her command.

'The next day I awoke, after a long, deep sleep, to find the sun high in the sky. There was no sign of bedding and the floor of the cave, far from being soft, was rugged and strewn with pebbles, but I had slept as well and warmly as in the room I once shared with my mother in my beloved native place, now a thousand *li* away. While I was washing in a nearby stream, a train of mules came down the track, driven by three mounted *lo-fu*. I easily persuaded one of these mule-drivers to sell me some cold steamed bread – he would have given it without payment, I am sure – and, with his help, I was able to rejoin my party by noon the following day.

'For more than a year I believed I had been saved by St Bernadette, though I could not account for her extreme youthfulness and Chinese appearance. Then, one day, I happened to take shelter from the rain in a disused temple not far from Chengtu and there, in a small chapel, I came upon a faded fresco showing Kuan Yin clad in a simple robe of blue cotton without her usual ornaments. Seated by the ocean, she was attended as usual by Shan Ts'ai and Lung Nü. In great astonishment, I recognised in Lung Nü my "Bernadette"! Even the blue dress and white trousers were the same, but now there were no jewels clasped about her throat. Thinking about those jewels roused a memory of a similar picture that used to hang in my mother's bedroom, showing both Kuan Yin and Lung Nü adorned with splendid ornaments. So that was it! You could say that the lady who saved my life on that freezing night was neither Bernadette nor Lung Nü, just a childhood memory lighting up a fear-crazed mind. And you would be right – partly! Still, childish memories do not guide people to unknown caves, make rocks and pebbles become fine mattresses, conjure *pei-wos* from the air or drive away deadly cold.

'Yes, in a way you would be right. It *was* that memory. It was also Lung Nü herself, sent out of pity by Kuan Yin. Having since then studied the profound Mahayana doctrine of Mind Only, I accept no contradiction between those two. Driven to the edge of reason, I sought divine aid, and divine aid came *instantly* – in a form that accorded with the contents of my mind.

It was as a mental apparition that Lung Nü appeared and brought from my mind the warmth and comfort that made me physically able to withstand great cold. Would you dare say that was not a miracle wrought by the Bodhisattva I had worshipped as a child? All miracles are so – working through mind. True, the Bodhisattva did not come herself. Having too much delicacy to appear before someone calling on a foreign goddess, she sent Lung Nü who could be taken for the child saint I was expecting. Attributing my good fortune to the marvellous workings of my own mind and accepting it as the intervention of the Bodhi-sattva are two ways of expressing the same truth.'

I have often pondered on the mineralogist's wisdom-opening experience. His penetrating understanding of it explains many similar occurrences, bridging the gap between magical and psychological. Years later, I chanced to hear – at second hand – another story, different in purport, but also illustrating the identity of miraculous intervention from 'within' and 'without' the mind. To understand what the narrator tells us, one must know that, whereas Kuan Yin, though often depicted as a member of a trinity with the celestial Buddha Amitābha in the centre and Kuan Yin and Ta Shih-Chih Bodhisattvas standing on either hand, is also worshipped independently by millions, this is not the case with Ta Shih-Chih. The latter seems to have faded from human consciousness, being rarely invoked in his own right. I am told the narrator was a very old gentleman called Mr Ch'ên, who had spent the last forty years of his life as a recluse.

'In my young days, preparing for the imperial civil service examinations was, for cultivated youths, the most important thing in life. Everything depended on success – not just rank and wealth, but the honour brought to one's family and the power to serve society effectively. You cannot imagine how hard we used to work at the ancient classics, straining our eyes through reading late into the night by the pitiful glimmer of a wick floating in a saucer of oil. No wonder so many of us became stooped early in life with all that poring over books! For me and my four brothers it was especially bad. My father, who loved the Buddhist sutras even more than the Confucian classics, made us spend much time on those as well! I do not know whether we grudged the extra burden more or less than we came to love the splendour, vastness and depth of their philosophy. "You must", my father often said, "pursue these studies until the meaning of the four characters FEI K'UNG CHIH K'UNG (voidness of the non-void) is as clear to you as the orb of the sun blazing down from a cloudless autumn sky."

'On some nights when I was especially weary, I liked to imagine that the compassionate Kuan Yin appeared before me in the library in a blaze of light. This never failed to wipe away my fatigue, making me as alert as in the mornings. Afterwards I could read the sutras quickly, easily and with greater understanding. I do not say that I truly saw her, unless dimly with my mind's eye, but I knew when and how sweetly she smiled or when she was displeased with a feeling I sometimes had that reading so many sutras was an intolerable chore. My fourth brother, who was sickly and the only one of us to fail the examinations, was extremely fond of me. When we were alone, we put aside the formality that had to be shown in public by juniors to seniors, even brothers almost of an age. Once when I had been describing what I liked to call the Bodhisattva's personal manifestations to me, he said, laughing: "How you flatter yourself, Second Brother. Such things don't happen. If they do, why is it always Kuan Yin and never Ta Shih-Chih who appears? The picture in our shrine-room contains both of them; they get the same amount of incense, bowing and the rest. Why doesn't Ta Shih-Chih do his share of healing you? It is because you forget him that he plays no part in your imagination – for it *is* imagination, whatever you say."

'His words set me thinking. I did not agree with his main point, but he had made me feel guilty towards Ta Shih-Chih Bodhisattva, to whom none of us paid reverence except as one of three. I began offering him special prayers. For several months I never went to sleep at night without first sitting cross-legged on my bed and visualising Ta Shih-Chih. But when I invoked him instead of Kuan Yin, there was no result. Never any result at all. At last I spoke of this to my father. Unable to explain, he sent me off to a monastery lying a few *li* beyond the city wall and overlooking a stream bordered with ancient willows – Kuan Yin's emblem. On learning why I had come, the elderly Tripitaka Master who presided there smiled and said: "You alone cannot evoke him."

' "You mean, Venerable, that the Bodhisattvas are merely forms in people's minds?" I protested, full of wonder to hear a monk speak so. Seeing him vigorously shake his head, I went on: "If they are real, what need of many minds to give them power to appear?"

' "What an ignorant young scholar you must be!" he answered, laughing. "Surely you know there *are* not many minds—just Mind. All the Buddhas and Bodhisattvas, all the myriad objects exist in this one Mind. How could it be otherwise? What is in your mind is naturally in Mind itself; even so, until you have dissipated the great mountains of obscurations constructed by karma earned in previous lives, you will not have the power to call forth a response to the feeble thoughts you put there. With Kuan Yin, the case is otherwise because so many millions of beings invoke her. Now do you understand?"

' "Venerable Sir, this worthless disciple can catch something of the profound purport of your enlightening teaching," I answered formally, though by no means sure I did. Satisfied, he raised his tea-cup in dismissal.

'That night I sat up later than any of my brothers. The little library-boy, who had orders from my father to stay within call until the last of us had handed him the books that needed putting away, replenished my tea-pot three times before I remembered to tell him to go off to bed, promising to put the flimsy volumes very carefully away in their blue boxes with my own hands. No sooner had the child walked off sleepily than the far end of the dimly lit library was illumined by a softly brilliant radiance and, as I fell to my knees, a slim, majestically tall, richly garbed figure, whom I took to be Kuan Yin was manifested in the centre of that circle of very bright but not dazzling light. The garments of the two Bodhisattvas being similar except for the head-dress, it took me a few moments to recognise Ta Shih-Chih encircled by a nimbus of golden flame.

' "Old Two," he announced in a thrillingly beautiful voice, but addressing me informally by the nickname used by my father and uncles, "the Venerable Tripitaka Master erred. Know that your mind is in itself immeasurable, the container of a myriad myriad universes, each of them vast beyond your comprehension. All the illimitable power that exists in those myriads of universes would be yours in full, if you had wisdom enough to use it. The same is true of every sentient being. Because your faith in me was not well developed, I have come to you always as Kuan Yin – not as I am now. Can you suppose we are two? *Two* in the great Mind where no two exist? Can a Bodhisattva feel wounded by neglect for as long as any other Bodhisattva is called upon? Not to speak of Bodhisattvas, when a single bee sucks honey, all beings in the myriad myriad universes suck honey; when a worm is crushed, all beings in those universes are crushed. Remember the source of all power lies within yourself and cease this foolish longing to behold mere manifestations."

'The lovely vision faded and was gone. Since then, I have never dared to call upon such beings, except as it should be done during meditation. Seeking from them power beyond the infinite power of our own mind, which is limited only by our own dark karmic obstructions, is like what the sutras call "looking for a head upon your head"! When, at those previous times, Kuan Yin assuaged my fatigue, it was because my mind willed that fatigue away, but needed the stimulation of the Bodhisattva's presence to function thus.

'Believe me, the Bodhisattvas are as real as earth and sky and have infinite power to aid beings in distress, but they exist within our common mind, which, to speak the truth, is itself the *container* of earth and sky.'

Both the mineralogist's story and old Mr Ch'ên's illustrate a concept not easy to grasp and perhaps not fully graspable until Enlightenment is won; but they do make it clear that, when Kuan Yin is regarded by some as a mental creation and by others as a being hardly distinguishable from a goddess, there is no question of the one view being right, the other wrong. She is both an abstraction and a goddess; how one sees her depends upon one's expectation and attitude of mind. All such mental attitudes, though one may think of them as 'higher' or 'lower' in the sense of exhibiting more or less wisdom and understanding, are probably so far from the ultimate truth that differences in one's level of wisdom becomes negligible. Nor

is it certain that to perceive a Bodhisattva as a god- or goddess-
like being does in fact demonstrate a lower degree of wisdom.
All talk of high and low, except in relative and provisional con-
texts, is beside the point.

> To the frogs in a temple pool
> The lotus-stems are tall;
> To the Gods of Mount Everest
> An elephant is small.

Chapter 3

Kuan Yin's Indian and Tibetan Genesis

World-Honoured Lord and Perfect One,
I pray thee now declare
Wherefore this holy Bodhisat
Is known as Kuan Shih Yin
                                        Lotus Sūtra

When the Red tide swept over China, Buddhism was not the universal faith there, as it is in Thailand and some other countries. Perhaps one Chinese in ten was Buddhist and, even then, not exclusively so in the sense of rejecting other religions. The educated classes, with only a fair number of exceptions, tended to be Confucian, following an agnostic ethical tradition that looked askance upon religious manifestations going beyond reverence for Heaven (as a moral principle or natural force) and performing memorial rites for the spirits of the ancestors. The ordinary people worshipped ten thousand gods whom they envisaged as resembling humans, though existing on a much grander scale. In the popular mind, Kuan Yin stood apart from those thronging deities only on account of her ineffable sweetness and merciful disposition; Bodhisattvas were not conceived by the uninstructed as differing from the gods in kind. The picture that emerges from the last story in the previous chapter reveals her as she appeared to the relatively small number of highly educated Chinese Buddhists. Having seen her thus, we must now examine her Indian origin and account for the strange fact that, though once identical with the male Bodhisattva,

Avalokita, she has long been depicted in China and neighbouring countries in womanly form.

It is possible that confusion in the popular mind between Bodhisattvas and local gods and goddesses permitted Miao Shan, a legendary Chinese princess with extraordinary compassion, to become assimilated to Kuan Yin, but personally I doubt if this assimilation took place until after the Bodhisattva had come to be regarded as female. In any case, when considering Kuan Yin in the light of orthodox Buddhism, we can disregard the Miao Shan accretions.

The sutras introduced from India account metaphorically for the origin of the various Bodhisattvas. Thus, it is written that Avalokita, bearing a lotus flower, was born from a ray of light that sprang from Amitābha Buddha's right eye; and that this miraculously born being straightway uttered the syllables OM MANI PADME HŪM. This is perhaps a poetic way of saying that Avalokita is a secondary emanation of the energy of compassion and that this is the mantra by which she should be invoked.

As Avalokita was widely venerated in India during the centuries when the University of Nalanda was at the height of its glory, it came about that his worship spread to Tibet in the seventh century AD as soon as Buddhism was introduced there by Padma Sambhava (the Lotus-Born Sage), fondly known as the Precious Guru. Before long Avalokita Bodhisattva was adopted as Tibet's tutelary deity and his mantra achieved wide popularity. By most Tibetans he came to be regarded as the Buddha's earthly representative and as chief guardian of the Dharma (Sacred Doctrine) until the advent of Maitraya Buddha in the aeon next to come. They never depict him or visualise him in female guise and, quite recently, His Holiness the Dalai Lama (who, as an emanation of Avalokita, should surely be a great authority on the subject) informed me that it would be thought wrong to do so by Tibetans.

When, as early as the first century AD, the practice of invoking Avalokita first reached China, no one thought of depicting him as female; moreover, the Chinese pilgrims Fa Hsien and Hsüan Tsang, who visited India in the fifth and seventh centuries respectively, record no such depictions either in India or China. Yet, by the twelfth century, female images of the Bodhisattva

were well-nigh universal both in China and Japan. Why? The
evidence of scholars sheds no light; their estimates of the date
at which the first of these female images appeared vary from
the seventh to thirteenth centuries! Not much credence is given
to the one or two people who aver that such images were worshipped in India and Nepal *before* this happened in China; and,
when the cult of Avalokita (under the name Lokeśvara) spread
from India to Champa and Cambodia in the ninth and tenth
centuries, his form was still male – as it is in Tibet and Mongolia
to this day. No, the change seems to have occurred in China
itself, certainly not much earlier than the eighth century or
much later than the eleventh.

There are good psychological grounds for envisaging compassion in womanly form; but, though these must certainly
have exercised their influence, they do not, I think, provide the
whole solution. The Saddharma Pundarika Sūtra affirms that,
of Avalokiteśvara's 337 earthly incarnations, *all were male*
and all human except for one. (This refers to the occasion
when the Bodhisattva was incarnated as the Balāka horse and
rescued an incarnation of the future Buddha from a horde
of Rākshāsha demons who were besetting him in alluring
female guise.) Bearing in mind that what is said of Avalokita
in the Lotus Sūtra merely credits him with the *ability* to
assume female form if need be and does not affirm that he
ever underwent rebirth as a woman, the conundrum may
be stated thus:

Avalokita's form is male;

Kuan Yin has for centuries been conceived of in female form;

Yet Avalokita and Kuan Yin are respectively Indian and
Chinese names for the same being.

Surely something is amiss?

To my mind, Mr P'an was right in supposing that the solution involves an Indo-Tibetan tertiary embodiment of compassion, Tara, a beautiful female divinity able to manifest herself
in twenty-one different forms for the sake of succouring sentient
beings. 'Born of a tear shed by Avalokita in sorrow for the world'
(that is to say, emanating from the compassionate Bodhisattva),
she is immensely popular in Tibet and Mongolia where her
devotees credit her with two main functions: rescuing beings
from present woes and assisting them to rid themselves of

the delusions binding them to samsara. But those are the very functions attributed to Kuan Yin!

Now Tara is not widely known in China or Japan (except among people familiar with the Tibetan tradition) and few Tara effigies are to be found there. Yet such an attractive being and one supported by sound canonical backing would surely have been eagerly welcomed, had not some other means of portraying compassion and its liberating powers in womanly form been devised. In my view, that is exactly what happened! The Chinese have always been disposed to envisage friendly divinities in idealised human form. As amusingly illustrated by one of the stories that follows, they do not feel at home with the multi-armed, multi-headed representations so dear to the Indian heart. Alas, all Avalokita's forms are inclined to be bizarre; now he appears with eleven heads to symbolise simultaneous perception of suffering and a thousand arms to succour the victims, now with three heads side by side, or with one head but four arms, and so on. To the humanistic Chinese, such forms were alien and unsuited to the portrayal of the yearning compassion a mother feels for her child. The lovely Tara, appearing now as a sweet-faced matron, now as a winsome maiden, would seem infinitely more appealing to the Chinese mind. For religious reasons, Chinese Buddhists could hardly reject (!) worship of the Bodhisattva Avalokita; on the other hand, since the forms taken by deities depend somewhat upon the meditator and the artist, there could be no objection to visualising Avalokita in a form similar to Tara's; and, if that were done, what need of both embodiments? So the two became one, thus preparing the way for the assimilation of Princess Miao Shan – a compassionate being enjoying the rank of goddess.

All of this may seem a private rationalisation, unsubstantiated. But there *is* persuasive evidence, as I was recently able to confirm. Visiting Japan this year at the time when the beauty of the hardy plum-blossom seen against a background of snow gives place to the fragile cherry-blossom, I chanced upon three early paintings of Kuan Yin, or Kwannon-Sama as she is known in that country. For several reasons there could be no doubt that the figure depicted *was* Kuan Yin, but her posture and the mudras formed by the fingers of both hands were those of Tara! Moreover, in the British Museum there is a painting in which

Diagram 1: *Genesis of the Female Representation of Kuan Yin*

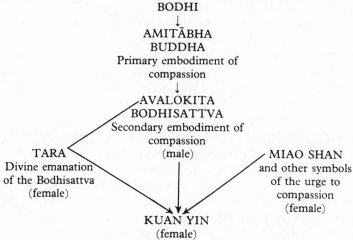

Diagram 2: *Esoteric Significance of that Genesis*

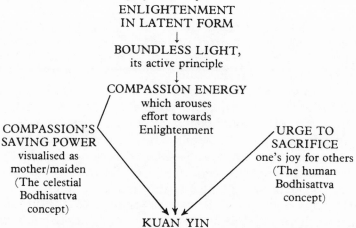

the central figure is clearly that of Kuan Yin, for she is accompanied by her Chinese disciples, Shan Ts'ai and Lung Nü, but again her posture is Tara's! Clearly these paintings belong to an era when the forms of Tara and Kuan Yin began to merge.

Viewed esoterically, the sex attributed to celestial Bodhisattvas is unimportant, since they are regarded as meditation forms not of *beings* but of what might be called cosmic forces.

To scholars and art-lovers, on the other hand, the details of iconography are of great significance. I shall be delighted if my interpretation of a puzzling enigma stimulates further study of early paintings and statues of Kuan Yin to determine more precisely when a change in the sex attributed to her took place.

Kuan Yin, though she has assimilated Tara (and Miao Shan), retains in the minds of her Chinese devotees full identity with Avalokita, so what is said in the sutras about him is, as it were, said of her. That Bodhisattva, as we have seen, is credited with having taken birth in a ray that sprang from the right eye of Amitābha Buddha, so he was presumably a celestial Bodhisattva from the first. On the other hand, the Sūrangama Sūtra relates the story of his Enlightenment in a way which suggests that he did not attain Bodhisattvahood until later. How the two accounts are reconciled I do not know, but the passage in the sutra has a bearing on Kuan Yin's name, Hearer-of-Cries, for it has much to do with the faculty of hearing.

It opens with the Bodhisattva testifying, before a great assembly of beings human and divine presided over by the Buddha, how, many aeons previously, he had attained Enlightenment through meditation on sound. Mentally detaching hearing from its object and then eliminating both those concepts, he had at first perceived that both disturbance and stillness are illusory and next came to realise the non-existence even of that rarified perception. 'As non-existent, both subject (hearer or hearing) and object (sound) are merged in the Void and awareness of voidness becomes all-embracing. When awareness of both existence and non-existence vanishes, Nirvāna supervenes.' Thus Enlightened, Avalokita (Kuan Yin) acquired two merits – the profound compassion that proceeds from Bodhi and sympathy with every kind of being floundering in samsara's ocean of delusion. Moreover, it is recorded that he attained the power of manifesting himself in thirty-two bodily forms, the better to succour different kinds of beings, and also the power to bestow fourteen kinds of fearlessness. All were fruits of Enlightenment attained by using 'illusory hearing' to develop 'Absolute Hearing'. When the Bodhisattva had spoken, the assembly agreed that, of the twenty-five methods for controlling mind which they were then debating, meditation on the process of hearing was best suited to untrained minds.

Ch'an (Zen) Masters sometimes quote this passage in relation to the koan method of meditation which employs verbal formulas, and the same is true of Masters belonging to the Pure Land Sect, since the faculty of hearing is intimately connected with the practice of concentrating on 'the sacred name'.

Like Amitābha Buddha, from whom he emanates, Avalokita is cherished on account of his vow to renounce Nirvāna's final peace for as long as there are sentient beings still lost amidst samsara's ocean. To believers, this is a stupendous vow, for it binds one to samsara for incalculable aeons. No wonder Avalokita (Kuan Yin) is adored by millions! Even so, humans, being as they are, most often enlist the Bodhisattva's aid in banishing some immediate affliction rather than in escaping from samsara's toils, even though the Buddhists among them must be aware that, until samsara is transcended, afflictions are bound to fall as copiously as rain!

Another sutra pertaining to Avalokita is much more deeply metaphysical and accounts for the reverence paid to him by the learned. Many Buddhists in China and Japan solemnly undertake to recite this Heart of Highest Wisdom Sūtra every day of their lives. Though but a single paragraph in length, it sets forth the quintessence of the entire body of 'Wisdom Teachings' which are elsewhere contained in verses running into hundreds of pages. Tersely it demolishes the ultimate delusion, the error of errors, the basic cause of our wandering aeon upon aeon from birth to death and death to rebirth—*belief in a real and permanent ego*. Not until the illusory nature of the ego is actually perceived can Enlightenment be won and Nirvāna's peace attained! In order to shock the hearer into sudden apprehension of this truth, what is said to Kuan Tzû-Tsai (a name for Kuan Yin) in the sutra *apparently* demolishes, blow by blow, the most widely known, revered and fundamental of all the previous teachings of the Buddha. But, whereas, to a traditionally minded Buddhist hearing it for the first time, its impact must be immense and horrifying until he suddenly grasps the underlying import, to someone unacquainted with Buddhist doctrine the text by itself might seem quite tame. So, with a view to giving at least a hint of its dramatic quality, I present it somewhat in the form in which it is expounded before assemblies of laymen by learned Tripitaka Masters. Imagine, then, a thin, grey-robed, shaven-headed figure seated cross-legged on his preaching throne, eyes alight with eagerness to communicate a truth of supreme importance to those with ears to hear. Placing his hands palm to palm, he first intones the sutra's name: 'Mahāprajñāpāramitā Hsin Ching!' (Sūtra of the Heart of Highest Wisdom!). Then, starting to speak in gentle tones which grow louder and more forceful as he proceeds, he says:

'Disciples of the Buddha, as you know well, the Blessed·One has taught that there is no self, that each living being is no more than a conglomeration of five skandhas (aggregates) – form, sensation, perception, discrimination and consciousness of these. But hear now the higher teaching he proclaimed in the Heart Sūtra for men and women with deep understanding: *"Kuan Tzû-Tsai Bodhisattva, while engaged in deep practice of the Highest Wisdom, perceived that all the five aggregates are void, and thereby passed beyond all forms of suffering."* The Compassionate Bodhisattva reached supreme attainment by recognising that even the five aggregates have no reality, being but bubbles, dreams, mirages. Herein lay her supreme wisdom. *"O Sariputra,"* continued the Blessed One, addressing his disciple, *"form differs not from void, nor void from form. Form IS void; void IS form. With sensation, perception, discrimination and consciousness it is the same. Sariputra, all these are marked by emptiness, neither coming into being nor ceasing to be, neither foul nor pure, neither increasing nor diminishing."* You have learnt, too, that beings and objects are taught by the Buddha to derive their appearances from a combination of eighteen "sense-realms", meaning the six organs of sense (including mind), the six kinds of sense perception and the six forms of consciousness to which these give rise, but in the Heart Sūtra the Blessed One announces: *"Therefore within the void there is no form, no sensation, perception, discrimination or consciousness; no eyes, ears, nose, tongue, body or mind; no form, sound, smell, taste, touch or thought; nor any of the others from eye-consciousness to mind-consciousness."* Such was the deep perception of the Bodhisattva Kuan Yin which won the Blessed One's praise.

'You have heard that beings must suffer birth after birth in samsara because bound by a twelvefold chain of causation, leading from primordial ignorance, through becoming and the other links to decay and death, and thence round and round again, but in the Heart Sūtra the Blessed One proclaims: *"There is neither ignorance nor extinction of ignorance, nor any of the others down to decay and death."* You all know well the Four Noble Truths; first, that existence is inseparable from suffering, including frustration, discontent, grief, pain, bereavement and so forth; second, that suffering has for its cause inordinate desire; third, that the remedy is cessation from inordinate desire; fourth, that this remedy is effected by treading the Noble Eightfold Path. But the Heart Sūtra proclaims: *"There is no suffering, no cause, no remedy, no Path (thereto)."* You have heard that through wisdom is Nirvāna attained, but the Sūtra says: *"There is no wisdom, no attainment. Because there is nothing to be attained, Bodhisattvas relying on this Highest Wisdom"*, of knowing there is *no* wisdom, *no* attainment, *"are free from hindrances of mind. Being rid of these hindrances, they have no fear, are free from all upsets and delusions, and in the end attain Nirvāna. It is by relying on this Highest Wisdom that all Buddhas of the past, the present and the future achieve Supreme Enlightenment."*

'Why does the Blessed One thus refute the core of his own doctrine? Does he not in this very sutra negate the foundations of everything he taught? Ah, but, for as long as you remain at the level of ordinary consciousness, for as long as you are still deluded by the differentiated realm of form into believing in the reality of the self, you must abide by those teachings without fail. Only when you reach the high level of perception attained by the Bodhisattva Kuan Yin will those teachings lose their validity for you. Only when your perception soars so high that you perceive with full clarity the voidness of absolutely everything there is, will you be able to understand that even the Blessed One's own teachings are ultimately void, since there is no entity, no concept whatsoever that is not void in its own nature. In that profound sense, there truly cannot be Nirvāna or any beings to attain it! When understanding dawns, you will know that ordinary teachings, no matter how exalted, must be laid aside, for how could Nirvāna – that pure state beyond being and non-being – be accessible to those who cling to differentiated concepts, however holy? To use the concluding words of the Heart Sūtra – *"Therefore do we know that the Highest Wisdom is a great and sacred mantra, a great mantra of knowledge, a mantra unsurpassed, unequalled. It can terminate all suffering truly and unfailingly. Therefore utter this Mantra of Highest Wisdom thus – Gatê, gatê, pāragatê, pārasamgatê, bodhi, svāhā!"* (Gone, gone, gone beyond, wholly gone beyond! Enlightenment! Svāhā!)

'Ah, but what is meant by *uttering* this mantra? It is not a matter of reciting a few syllables in the language of the Brahma-country. "Uttering" means "living" the mantra by perceiving the voidness of all concepts, entities and beings without one single exception. Only when their voidness dawns brightly upon the eye of your mind may you abandon the teachings given before and rest in the brilliant, unwavering perception of pure, boundless, shining void!'

This exposition of the profound perception attained by Kuan Yin, or Avalokiteśvara as the Sanskrit version of the sutra has it, carries us into the realm of highest mysticism, and helps to explain the reverence felt for that Bodhisattva in Tibet, China and Japan, not only by the common people but by mystics and scholars as well; for, according to the sutra, it was Kuan Yin (Avalokita) who first penetrated beyond the exoteric teachings of the Buddha and caused the Blessed One to reveal their meaning at a level infinitely more profound. However, what is said here needs to be rounded off by the kind of story that circulates about the Bodhisattva at the popular level; it would not do to suppose that mystics and sages are extremely common among the Far Eastern peoples. For every individual able to understand the inner meaning of the Heart Sūtra, there must be a hundred who revere the Bodhisattva for very different reasons. As this chapter relates to the Indian genesis of that being, I have chosen the only folk story I know relating to Avalokita, that is to say the male aspect. Tales of Tara and the womanly Kuan Yin aspect are very much easier to come by; for, among Tibetans, with whom the original Indian tradition still lingers, Avalokita is revered as too high a being to be thought of as playing the kindly pranks dear to Tara or manifesting himself quite as readily as the gentle Chinese Kuan Yin. This reflects what was said earlier about the streams of compassion energy becoming more tangible with distance from the source. The one story about Avalokita which has stayed in my memory has just a touch of harshness. Most Bodhisattvas (including Kuan Yin in her Chinese form and even the smiling

Tara) are credited with showing stern displeasure upon occasion, though this is rare and, when it becomes necessary for such beings to seem harsh, they punish solely to teach wisdom to those chastised. There is no resemblance to Jehovah's proclivity for vengefulness, no calling on people to present their sons as burnt offerings, even though it be only to test their obedience; a Bodhisattva's wrath is directed always at error itself, never at errant beings. The story, of which I have had to fill in most of the details, as I recall only its essentials, runs as follows:

In the lovely Blue Lake province of China, where the settled inhabitants are mostly of Tibetan stock and Mongol nomads graze their flocks in lonely pastures, few Chinese used to live outside the cities and it sometimes happened that an isolated Chinese peasant family would be found tilling a few *mou* of land in a vicinity where they and their neighbours had no common language. So it was with the Chiangs, new arrivals from Szechuan, a family consisting of an elderly couple, their two sons and daughters-in-law and a small brood of grandchildren. About an hour's journey from their farm stood a Tibetan village clustering around a temple to Avalokita wherein stood a tall image with eleven heads and a thousand arms. Though the Chiangs sometimes visited this temple when attending the village market nearby, it never entered their heads that the bizarre-looking statue represented a form of their beloved Kuan Yin! The women-folk, especially, were awed by its appearance; ignorant of the comforting meaning of its symbolism and quite unable to question the Tibetans about it, they supposed the heads betokened power to see the evil in every heart; the hands, power to inflict severe retribution.

'What sort of people can our neighbours be?' exclaimed the voluble old lady. 'Imagine adoring such a god and not being upset by the sight of all those heads and their staring eyes!' Lowering her voice, she added: 'I've a queer sort of feeling that god only likes Tibetans. They say those people want to drive us Chinese from the province. Anyone can see they think they own it. If we wake up one day with our throats cut, don't say I didn't warn you. If they haven't done it already, it's because they are waiting for a sign from the god!'

'I hope you're right,' remarked her husband drily. 'If they

wait for that, our great-grandsons will be living here safely. An ordinary household cat can give a signal for revolt more easily than a many-headed image.'

'Hush!' exclaimed the old woman, shocked. 'The surest way of stirring up gods and demons is to make fun of them.'

'May Old Eleven Heads do his worst!' cried Chiang, and went out laughing.

Half out of her mind with fear of the consequences of this blasphemy, Mrs Chiang got not a wink of sleep. Up before dawn, she cooked some food-offerings for the maligned deity and, as the sun rose, set off with her younger daughter-in-law for the temple. Pausing to buy the best incense in the outer courtyard, they entered the shrine-hall and, more than a trifle awed, presented their offerings – a fine roast chicken, pig's knuckles and a few thimblefuls of Szechuanese *ta-ch'iu* wine. While they were arranging them upon the altar, a Tibetan monk happened to come in. Staring at the altar in astonished disbelief, he shouted to the women to be off with their impure offerings. For demons and guardian deities one provided meat and wine as a matter of course, but for the compassionate Avalokita!!! As these stupid women made no effort to comply, he resorted to violent gestures. The offending offerings were hurriedly removed.

'You see!' cried Mrs Chiang indignantly, the moment they were safely outside. 'Now you know what I mean about cutting our throats. That sort of god is bound to enjoy roast chicken and those barbarians are afraid we shall win his favour and protection. Somehow we've got to get the chicken and pig's legs to him – never mind about the wine – and then we'll be safe.'

It is not related how they managed it, only that baskets of animal flesh were found the next day, tucked beneath the trailing ends of long silk scarves suspended from some of Avalokita's thousand arms.

On the way home, Mrs Chiang was in the best of humours. Whenever the two women encountered parties of Tibetans, they could hardly suppress their merriment at the thought that these barbarians were blissfully unaware that a couple of defenceless Chinese women had stolen a march on them.

'Be sure it will work,' the old woman chuckled. 'Long before they discover the offerings, the gods will have inhaled their essence. Who cares what they do with the flesh and bones?'

On a moonless night later in the month, masked men in bulky Tibetan robes descended upon the farm-house and, having driven the family out into the night, burnt it to the ground. The Chiangs fled to the district town, where they pressed the magistrate to punish the miscreants, but obtained no satisfaction. With only a meagre force of Chinese soldiers in the neighbourhood, the magistrate had no wish to stir up a local uprising. 'What is more,' he sternly told the Chiangs, 'you have yourselves to blame. Who in all the lands under heaven would offer the flesh of slaughtered animals to Kuan Yin?'

'That fearful-looking – I mean, that stern and noble-looking image, Kuan Yin's?' shrieked old Mrs Chiang. 'Oh what a terrible sin! How could I know? Now we shall all end up in hell!'

It is to be hoped that her family were able to convince her that a sin committed in ignorance would never bring down retribution from so compassionate a goddess as Kuan Yin; but what happened to the family is not recorded. This is a Tibetan story and the Chiangs, having played their part, are allowed to fade out at this point.

Meanwhile, Avalokita Bodhisattva was displeased.

The winter that year was severe and, for an inexplicable reason, the temple's supporters were much less lavish than usual with their offerings. Hunger drove the two monks and three novices to the district township where they applied to the magistrate for relief.

'What are your affairs to me?' demanded the 'Father-and-Mother of the District'. 'No state of famine has been declared. No considerable body of people have failed to make provision for the winter. Your unenviable condition is a private matter with which the Government can have no concern. Besides' – he added slyly – 'would you like everyone to know that Tibetans treat Buddhist monks so shabbily that they have to turn to the Chinese authorities to keep them from hunger? If a story like that got about, you people from the pious land of Bod would lose a lot of face, don't you think?'

Abashed, the monks strode away and, the Bodhisattva relenting somewhat, they soon found a Tibetan merchant willing to lodge them for some days. For the rest of the winter, they lived precariously, staying with one family after another, never failing to receive due respect, but seldom much generosity. Times were hard. When spring came, the little party returned to their temple and set about repairing the ravages caused by months of neglect. The offerings from round about kept them from actual want, but they seldom had a really satisfying meal.

Towards the end of spring came a minor festival in honour of Avalokita Bodhisattva. For once the eve was passed in a manner not demanded by custom. The chief monk, having long ago concluded that somehow or other they had incurred the Bodhisattva's displeasure, decreed a special ceremony of purification. Even hungrier than usual because the rite demanded previous abstinence, they sat facing each other, two on one side, three on the other, in front of the altar. Summoning the remains of their strength, they beat the drum, clashed the cymbals and chanted lustily, but the hearts of the younger ones especially were not in it. Then gradually the yogic rite wrought its spell and they were able to visualise, with the utmost clarity, white light streaming from a Buddha form mentally envisaged above their heads, entering their bodies and expelling through every pore and orifice a stream of filthy impurities which fell straight into the mouths of the hungry demons waiting for this horrid banquet in a hell-pit yawning beneath where they were sitting. Taken up with this inner vision, they were hardly aware of the great eleven-headed, thousand-armed statue which dominated the shadowed hall from behind an altar now laden with rows of butter-lamps and ritual *torma* offerings.

For a long space of time, all was well with them; but, as the bliss of meditation faded, they one by one became uneasily aware that something strange and wholly unconnected with their visualisation was taking place. Though the great doors were tight shut and no breeze could enter, there came a stirring and fluttering, a tinkling and clinking from the objects held in the statue's many hands. Soon the words of the mantra died upon their lips and they glanced fearfully at each other, their awe increasing every moment, for it was not to be denied that the statue had begun to glow with a soft light that was gradually increasing in intensity, and the broad chest beneath the gauzy silk brocades rose and fell as though in response to deep, calm breathing! The rays emanating from the Bodhisattva's person now formed an ever brighter halo and nimbus of coloured

flame! Greatly though they adored the Compassionate Avalokita, this manifestation of his actual presence was more chilling
than welcome and awe gave place to terror. Hurriedly they prostrated themselves, heads to the stone-flagged floor; and, as they
did so, a deep voice came echoing melodiously across the hall.

'O foolish and unheeding monks forgetful of your vow to
succour sentient beings and show compassion to one and all,
the season of my displeasure is at an end. It is well you had
the wit to purify yourselves of murky error. I have not punished
you severely as you deserved, but neither did I stay my hand
from chastising you enough to make you feel its weight, for you
will make no progress along the path until you have learnt that
they who seek compassion must themselves be compassionate
to every being alike without either chilliness or special favour –
still less vengefulness! Now the end of your lean days has come.
Tomorrow's festival will bring food-offerings in plenty. Be
grateful and henceforth be diligent not to incur my sorrow.
It will go ill with those who err a second time.'

These last words, uttered slowly in tones of solemn admonition, made the monks stare suspiciously at one another, supposing that one of them had done a great evil unknown to the
others. At last the Abbot, summoning courage, said fearfully:
'Compassionate Lord, we have tried to serve you well and keep
to the terms of our vow to pity all beings alike. Wherein lies
our error?'

'In you most of all,' the bell-like voice replied. 'Have you
so soon forgotten causing misery and loss to ignorant folk who
sought only to do well by bringing to my temple what they
believed to be the most acceptable of offerings?'

'B-but, Compassionate Lord,' stammered the Abbot in deep
distress, 'it was not we who burnt down their dwelling. It was
done without our knowledge and, when it became known to
us, we took those men to task.'

'Silence, old man,' answered the Bodhisattva chillingly. 'You
speak only of the effect. The cause lay with you, the monks and
novices of this temple. Who spread word of what those ignorant
people had done to show reverence to me? In what terms was
their folly made known? Who would have set fire to their dwelling if *you* had not incited them to wrath? Evil lies with those
who set an evil chain of causation in motion, not with those

caught up in the effects of the causes. Meditate on this. Should you forget, your penance will be memorable.'

Now were the monks abashed. As they bowed down in contrition, the breeze playing about the Bodhisattva's garments died away; the tinkling and clinking ceased; the bright rays were withdrawn, and all was as before. To calm themselves, the monks returned to their recitation of the mantra of purification with deep concentration. And so the night passed. In the morning, crowds of peasants, made joyful by the early promise of a rich harvest later in the year, came to the festival with offerings more generous than was customary on that occasion. Thenceforward the monks, full of holy inspiration, gave themselves to meritorious deeds and became renowned for kindness bestowed with firm impartiality. The fame of that temple spread far and wide and its supporters flourished.

Thus Avalokita as seen by the pious story-tellers of Tibet. As to Tara, it is said that she was born of a tear shed by Avalokita in pity for the sufferings of sentient beings. In appearance, she is far from awe-inspiring. The Chiang family would have had no difficulty in recognising *her* as a form of Kuan Yin, for she resembles an exceptionally lovely human being in everything but colour and splendour of her ornaments. Whether visualised as a sweet-faced matron or as a winsome sixteen-year-old maiden, she has two principal embodiments known as the Green Tara and the White. They are much alike except that, from her seat upon a moon disc supported by a giant lotus, the Green Tara extends one foot as though about to rise from meditation, whereas the White Tara sits in meditation posture and is further differentiated by having a visible 'wisdom eye' in the centre of her forehead as well as eyes set in the palms of each hand. With both forms, the head is charmingly inclined, the body a trifle arched so that the left shoulder is perceptibly higher than the right; one hand, held close to the heart, forms the mudra of protection and the other, resting lightly upon the knee, forms the gesture of bestowing gifts. A long-stemmed lotus rises from the crook of the left arm. Heavy ornaments of gold adorn the high-piled hair, throat, wrists and ankles; the filmy garments – bright gauzy silks fluttering from the shoulders and a series of many-hued silken skirts – leave the slender torso and smoothly rounded breasts uncovered in the manner of ancient India. The whole effect is so ravishing that she might well arouse the very passion she is frequently invoked to calm, were it not that she inspires the kind of exalted reverence a palace guard might be expected to feel for a young and lovely princess entrusted to his care. No doubt there have been palace guards who, placed in such circumstances, have had to dissemble a more earthly passion; not so with Tara, for she is imbued with the power to vanquish lust as easily as sorrow.

Though sweetly dignified when evoked during meditation, Tara's nature is as fun-loving and mischievous as that of any of the sixteen-year-old girls she so often resembles. Tibetans say she is sometimes to be seen seated tomboy-style astride a beam or roof-tree; she has been known to laugh gaily at things that strike her as ridiculous and to restrain thoughtless misbehaviour by uttering a well-timed 'Humph!' or scornful 'Really!' Altogether she is the most lovable of all the Buddhist deities, Kuan Yin included, except that they are really one; but, when she is seen as Kuan Yin, the tomboyishness is absent, for antics welcome to the fun-loving Tibetans are apt to strike the more staid Chinese as not entirely decorous in a goddess.

There is also a set of 'Twenty-One Taras', who are sometimes portrayed as identical with the Green Tara apart from their distinctive colours, but at other times with differences of facial expression and symbolic ornament. In the latter case, one of the Twenty-One may appear in the fierce daemonic form suited to encounters with the turgid powers of evil.

Lovable and deeply loved, Tara is close to the hearts of all Tibetan, Mongolian and Nepali Buddhists. Indeed, in the People's Republic of Mongolia, I often saw her image standing with Lenin's a little to one side, in the place of honour facing the doorway of a herdsman's *yurt* (tent)! Stories of her exploits, sometimes amusing always merciful, are legion and very similar in content to Chinese tales of Kuan Yin. Year after year new ones are heard in the most unlikely places. For instance, recently a Kargyupta monk from Nepal, who had spent some months among the mainly Chinese population of Ipoh, Malaysia, told me he had frequently been asked by hard-headed modern-minded businessmen to invoke Tara's assistance in such matters as persuading a run-away daughter to return home or a business partner to be less domineering – never, so he assured me, unsuccessfully. Tara is a newcomer among overseas Chinese communities, but they have only to know of her to enjoy invoking Kuan Yin in Tara form. However, in the context of the Bodhisattva's Indo-Tibetan progenitors, the two must be regarded as in some sense separate and it seems appropriate to select a typically Tibetan story of Tara's powers. It is one that seems to me especially touching.

Some years ago, there dwelt in a Himalayan hamlet a young couple who, with a child already stirring in the lady's womb, wrested a living from a rocky holding with soil so shallow that the barley they sowed could scarcely take root. Even in the best of years the crop was meagre and stunted. But above them rose the sky's azure dome and on all sides gleamed rocks of the 'five colours' interspersed in spring and summer with richly verdant patches of grass and wild flowers, so they could vividly imagine the beauty of Tara's sea-girt paradise. One year when people had incurred the mountain gods' displeasure, snow fell endlessly upon the fields, blizzards tore the roofs from the monastery in the lower valley and the mountain passes above were blocked for months on end. With the spring came floods that, besides sweeping away the shallow soil, caused the east wall of the young couple's house to crumble and drowned their only beast of burden – an aged, much-beloved yak. All that those two had struggled so long to build now vanished in the space of weeks like a beautiful dream from which the dreamer awakes to find himself in pitiable circumstances. With their granary empty, the last of the seed-corn consumed as food, their house falling about their ears and their patient yak gone the way of all sentient beings, they had nothing in the world but some ragged garments and a few old farm implements no one would care to buy.

'Pema,' sighed the husband, 'for us it is the end. In a year like this, even the monks will be hard put to it to live through to the next harvest. There must be many others living round about who are as much in need of charity as we, and, though our neighbours are kind, there is not a family within ten days' walk with food to spare. It is well our child is not yet born since we ourselves are going to die.'

'For shame, Norbu! You must be out of your senses to talk so wildly,' answered the young matron with spirit. 'You know well enough that Tara the Saviouress succours all who call upon her, heart full, mind one-pointed.'

'You women are all alike,' observed Norbu loftily, 'letting yourselves be taken in by fables. Did we or did we not burn incense upon the family altar every night for as long as there was incense to burn? Did we or did we not offer butter-lamps at a time when there was not butter enough to put in our own tea? Call on Tara, if you will. It can do neither good nor harm.'

'Indeed I shall call on her – and with faith enough for us both. Help will come and I shall wish to show our gratitude fittingly. Come now and join me in a solemn vow to present our son to the monastery when he is old enough to be admitted.'

'We'll do nothing of the kind,' her husband answered sourly.

'Why, Norbu? As you are sure we have no hope, such a vow should not trouble you at all. According to you, we shall both be dead and the child unborn, so what difference can it make?'

'Have it your own way. I'll join you if that's any comfort, but take care to inform the Precious Ones that our son will enter the monastery's service only if there can be no possible doubt that any help we receive comes from Tara. If aid comes owing to chance or accident, we shall owe Tara nothing. Agreed?'

So they made their vow, kneeling side by side before the household altar, Norbu growing restless as Pema's prayers went on and on, and staying on his knees only because he knew of nothing else to do but lie down and wait for death. While, towards the rite's end, they were reciting Tara's mantra for the second or third thousandth time, Pema envisaging the lovely haloed figure in her mind, there came a din of shouting and hammering on the door.

Horsemen, speaking in the uncouth accents of Kham, had come riding through the pass where deep snow had given way, to foaming cataracts. Though they had hoped for food and hot tea, these burly men were kind enough to take such viands as they had from their saddlebags and share them with the starving couple. From their talk it soon appeared that they were the remnant of a band of resistance fighters badly mauled by a detachment of the Chinese Red Army. On Norbu's eagerly agreeing to join them, they gave him a horse to share with Pema until, several days later, they were able to leave her with some distant maternal relatives who lived close to the Lhasa road.

In so doing they were just in time. No sooner had her husband ridden off with the others than her labour pains began and presently she was delivered of a sturdy son.

'O Dolma,' she whispered, calling Tara by that name, 'this boy is the fruit of your compassion. You know, dearest One, he is vowed to the service of the monastery. Teach him to be devout and deeply learned in our sacred *Chos* (religion).'

Two years later, Norbu, after many fearsome adventures, rejoined his wife and the three of them fled southwards into India, where they settled down in Darjeeling and learnt to earn a living by carpet-making. When the child was five, Pema said:

'Soon you must take him to the monastery in Kalimpong. Tell them he is vowed to the Three Precious Ones, ask formally for him to be admitted and enquire at what age he should be given into their care.'

'Fool!' shouted Norbu in a voice of fury. 'What had Tara to do with us? Those Khambas were already half way down from the pass before you as much as mentioned vowing our son to the monastery!'

'Yet they stopped at our wreck of a house instead of riding on to the monastery or the village store. It was Tara who guided them. There must be no thought of going back on our promise now that we are warm, comfortable, well fed and safe from the Chinese. Even you could not be so impious and ungrateful.'

As Norbu was obdurate and Pema could not arrange for the child to be admitted without the father's consent, her best resource lay with Tara. The next time her husband left her alone with the boy, she ran to light incense and cried fervently: 'Dolma, dearest One, I have not forgotten. This child *will* become a monk, I promise; but please do something to make it easy for us. You alone can smooth the way.'

That night, having made stormy love though still too angry to speak to her, Norbu fell asleep. Presently a bright light fell upon his eyes and, starting up in alarm, he beheld Tara seated negligently on the table, swinging her legs like a child with more energy than she knew what to do with. However, even as he leapt up to prostrate himself, her body began to glow with light. The window behind her was dissolved in these rays and, in its place, he saw the peak of a lofty hill covered with lush green grass wherein glittered innumerable points of light as though it were bestrewn with gems. Beyond and stretching to the horizon was an expanse of deep blue water capped by magnificent white waves which, breaking on the shore below, emitted rainbow-coloured clouds of spray. These clouds, rising to the hilltop, filled the air with millions upon millions of glittering particles like multi-coloured jewels. Meanwhile, the table had become a moon disc resting on a huge and many-petalled lotus, whereon Tara sat, still negligently and with the air of a young girl having fun, but now clad in shining silks and golden ornaments like the daughter of the Emperor of the Sky. She was smiling at him with a mixture of archness and contempt.

'Well, Norbu?' she enquired with a smile so dazzling that his heart almost burst with joy. 'Do you regret my saving you from death? Do you regret having the lovely Pema safely at your side? Do you regret having money for tea and as many of Pema's meat dumplings as you care to eat? Do you regret promising your son to the service of the Three Precious Ones?'

'No, no, no!' cried Norbu in an ecstasy of devotion. 'All shall be as the Excellent Dolma commands.'

'*Commands*, Norbu? *Did* I command you? If so, it is very strange, for commanding is not my way. Somehow I thought it was you and Pema who *prayed* for these things. I thought you *wished* me to protect you and cause you to prosper. Was it not so, Norbu? Can you provide your son with a better future than will be his as a pious and learned lama with perhaps hundreds of disciples? Just say, if you think you can.'

'No, no, no! Indeed I cannot! I shall take him to Kalimpong tomorrow – no, today at sunrise.'

'That is well, Norbu. A promise is a promise. You will be happy to watch your son grow up to be a help to others and a faithful guardian of our sacred *Chos*. Later he must live with his teachers, but no one will hinder your going to see him as often as you wish. Now get off your knees, Norbu, and sit facing me.'

Hastily he assumed the posture of meditation, but with his head reverently inclined, dazzled by her radiance. Then did a blinding ray shoot forth from Tara's heart and, entering through his crown, fill every part of his body with light whiter than snow or camphor dust. Cool was that ray, yet like a white-

hot molten stream it burnt away the effects of his karmic obscurations, bestowing ecstatic bliss. Then the vision faded, leaving
him seated cross-legged in the darkness close to the sleeping
Pema, to whom he longed to speak of the glory that had descended from Potala's peak.

The morning was not far advanced when he and his son,
Pemba, reached Kalimpong by the early bus. Hurrying to the
monastery, he implored the monks to accept *both* of them there
and then.

'Does the child have no mother?' asked the novice-master
gently. After enquiring in some detail into the whole affair, he
agreed to take the child but not the father. 'Since this is your
only son and he will be coming to us two years from now, you
had best go back and make other sons, for your wife's sake if
not your own. As for this boy, since he comes to us as a gift
from Tara, his name in religion will be one which carries that
meaning. I shall give some thought to it. Tell your wife, by
the way, that if she fervently whispers Tara's name when you
are making children together, you are sure to have a lovely,
high-spirited daughter. Be sure to call the child Tara – or
Dolma, if you prefer.'

Much of this beautiful story, if provided with a Chinese setting, could be related of Kuan Yin. There are hundreds of
stories about her so close in spirit to this one as to leave no room
for doubt that they are essentially one and the same being. Such
similarities are all the more striking in that few other figures
of the Mahayana Buddhist pantheon are sufficiently alike to
suggest different forms of the same being, except in the sense
that all of them are emanations whose ultimate source is the
Great Void – illimitable Mind.

Of the methods of invoking Tara, some are simple. Indeed,
she is said to respond upon the instant should one do no more
than cry aloud her name just once with heart-felt fervour,
though it is generally considered more effective to call aloud
her mantra – OM TARÉ TUTARÉ TURÉ SVĀHĀ! On the
other hand, mantras are held to be fully efficacious only when
one has mastered their use by frequent recitation accompanied
by the appropriate visualisation. Since, in the case of a sudden
emergency, there may not be time to enunciate all ten syllables,
some adepts are taught to use OM TARÉ TAM SVĀHĀ! upon

such occasions, TAM being the *bīja*- or seed-mantra that contains Tara's essence.

When the purpose is a more exalted one, that of making progress towards Enlightenment and attaining Tara-like power to succour sentient beings, a rite of visualisation is regularly performed to enable the meditator to draw upon and become absorbed by compassion's liberating power. The forms used for this rite vary from simple to elaborate, but essentially they are alike. After taking refuge in the Triple Gem (Buddha, Dharma and the Sacred Community), renewing one's vow to succour all sentient beings, offering salutation to Tara, confessing and abjuring shortcomings in this and previous lives, etc., one summons to mind a sacred syllable that seems to hang in the air on a level with the meditator's eyes. In a flash it is transformed into a lotus surmounted by the discs of sun and moon, whereon appears a second glowing syllable which instantly gives place to Tara's image. By the power of mantras, mudras and skilled visualisation, Tara is summoned to manifest herself within this image, which suddenly begins to shine with supernatural radiance. Hundreds of repetitions of the mantra follow and presently Tara contracts into a tiny being no larger than a thumb, but glowing like emerald fire. Entering the meditator's person by way of the secret gateway at the crown, she descends into his heart, causing his own body to contract in turn until each tiny figure is coterminous with the other and they are no longer two, but one. The meditator (or, as one may now say, Tara) continues to contract until nothing remains but a shining syllable that had first appeared sending forth rays from Tara's heart; this syllable now withdraws into itself until nothing whatever is left but the pure, undifferentiated brightness of the illimitable Void.

Some devotees, if their way of life is sufficiently stainless, are bold enough to retain Tara within themselves as they go about the business of the day (the harmless business of monks or recluses free from most occasions of error). With the passing of years, they become so closely identified with her that they noticeably take on some of her characteristics; perhaps even the facial contours undergo a change so that, as is the case with many saintly old lamas among Tibetans, they cease to be either distinctively male or female. Lost in the bliss of almost un-

ceasing meditation, such a person develops wisdom and compassion so profound that Enlightenment is won within a single
life-span; thereafter he enters upon the Bodhisattva's task of
succouring sentient beings, aeon upon aeon, throughout the
myriad world-systems of samsara.

As an example of the tales told of Tara, the story of Norbu
and Pema has one failing; it does not do justice to Tara's special
characteristic of impish humour. So, feeling sure Kuan Yin will
excuse me for keeping her off-stage a little longer (all the more
so as Tara is herself Kuan Yin in another form), I shall relate
another story which brings this humour out. I had it from a
Tibetan in Kalimpong and will try to tell it as he did.

'Near our village in Tibet there stood an isolated cottage
where lived an old fellow called Jigme. He was in his nineties
at the time, but hale enough for a thirty-year-old. As a boy I
would see him going up the path behind our monastery in all
kinds of weather, taking provisions to the cave of our local
hermit. His end, when it came, was sudden – two days of ailing
and he was gone with a smile. Since long before I came into
the world, he had been renowned as an eccentric, forever sing-
ing songs to Tara, making offerings to Tara, meditating on
Tara – always, always Tara. We boys used to make fun of him
among ourselves, for he reminded us of an elderly husband
making a terrible fuss of a teenage wife for fear she might run
off with someone else. Our elders thought the world of him and
the monks gave him a splendid send-off, banging away at their
drums and chanting for a good three days before taking his old
body up the mountain as his final offering to the birds and
beasts, who probably didn't mind its being a bit tough. When
we had got used to his being gone, we put him out of mind
most of the time, but we shall never forget the stories told about
him on the night before they took away his body.

'When young, Jigme had been noted for three things –
strength, good looks and a blazingly hot temper. As a petty
trader who had dealings with the monastery, he once got into
a scrap with the layman who worked as cook there. They'd been
drinking in the monastery kitchen – only *chang* probably, but
that can be strong enough. Without quite knowing how, Jigme
managed to kill the man and ran off leaving his body sprawled
across the kitchen flagstones. The authorities took as lenient

a view as they could and Jigme was sentenced to be locked up
in the monastery dungeon for a time. From the moment the
door clanged behind him, he started yelling like a madman and
battering the wood with his fists so that his shackles rang like
cymbals clashing. Just after nightfall when it was too early for
Jigme to think of sleep, a sudden silence fell and presently one
of the monks went down to see if the wretched man had injured
himself. No one who knew Jigme could imagine him just giving
up. On his way to the cell, the monk stopped short, having
caught the sound of voices. First came Jigme's voice saying
fiercely "Yes, yes. *All* my life, I promise." The answering voice
brought the old monk in the passage to his knees, forehead to
the ground. In tones gently mocking and yet of inconceivable
sweetness, someone replied: "Then see to it, Jigme dear. Otherwise you might be held to it in ways you would find uncomfort-
able." Who could doubt that those sweetly mocking tones were
Holy Tara's? Not daring to intrude, the old monk tremblingly
padded off in search of the Abbot.

'The next morning, Jigme was not to be found in his cell.
The door and window seemed much as usual, but the fetters
lying on his bed had been wrenched asunder like bits of dough-
cake. They found him later sitting dazed and peaceful in his
own cottage. Well, there was no question of dragging him back
and making him serve his sentence after that. Who would dare?
Yet there was plenty of excitement. The villagers kept peeping
through his window in the hope that Tara would appear
again. She did not, but she had earned Jigme such fame that
they made him chief contractor to the monastery and, doing
very well indeed, he gradually began to lose his new air of
peacefulness.

'Now and then business took him to a nearby township – oh,
not more than three days' ride from our village, if you had a
good horse like Jigme's. Once, while putting up at the inn there,
he got into a fight with a couple of men from Dergé. Felling
one with his great fist, he was about to assault the other when
a raggedly dressed girl came running in from no one quite knew
where, crying "Jigme dear, for shame! That's the way to mil-
dew good barley!" Then she was gone, but Jigme, trembling
like someone troubled by a ghost, dropped his hands and let
the second man from Derge give him a mighty trouncing that

left him unconscious on the floor. That was not the end of it, either. A consignment of barley he had bought for making *chang* for a monastery festival due in a few days turned out to be so damaged by a mysterious dampness that the Abbot ordered him to take it away and give him back his money!

'A year or so later, Jigme was defrauded in some way by a cloth merchant. Finding everyone agreed that he was in the right, he decided to press charges that were likely to cost the fellow more than he possessed. Some people thought him too ruthless towards a poor wretch with a family to support, so they tried to get him to withdraw or moderate the charges. Not Jigme! Off he rode with his man-servant to the district magistrate's seat, a place on the border of Kham where the authorities are Chinese. In the outskirts of the town, finding the way blocked by a clumsy carter, he raised his whip. Before the blow could fall, a young girl darted from the crowd, crying: "Take care your horse doesn't tire of carrying such an oaf!" By then the way was clear and Jigme pressed on at as fast a trot as the width of the street allowed. All of a sudden, a length of cloth hanging up in a dyer's yard billowed out in the wind. The horse shied and Jigme fell on his head heavily enough to crack his skull. By the time he had recovered from the accident, the cloth merchant had fled with his family to another neighbourhood. Nothing more was heard of the law suit.

'After that, all went well for several years until Jigme took it into his head to ride off with his man on a pilgrimage to Kumbum Monastery. At a wayside inn, he fell to quarrelling with some ruffians and drew his sword. They ran off, only to waylay him further along the road with a dozen or so mounted supporters. In the fight that followed, three of them were wounded before Jigme and his servant were secured. Maybe they had meant only to rob Jigme and give him a good beating, but their blood was up and it was decided to make an end of him. While preparations were going forward to "have a little fun" with the two captives, an elegant young man with pink cheeks and maiden-soft skin came galloping up, leading two spare horses on a rein. "Jigme, my dear, you are duller than a yak," cried a well-known voice. "Be sure this is the very last time." With these words, the youth drew a deep breath and, blowing it out effortlessly, caused the dust to rise in clouds. Yellow night engulfed the earth until long after the captives had ridden off to a place of safety.

'The Jigme who had left for that pilgrimage was not the same as the Jigme who returned. From Kumbum he brought back a precious statue of Tara made of alloy mixed with gold, and many pretty things for furnishing a shrine-room in her honour. Gradually relinquishing his trading ventures, he spent more and more time at home and soon turned into the pious recluse known to me in my boyhood. I suppose no one ever learnt the whole of the affair, but nobody doubts that Tara was involved at every stage. I should like to know why she favoured that ill-tempered young fellow more than any of the pious folk in our village. At some time in his childhood or soon after, he must have won her heart by some great deed of compassion which has never been recorded. I wish I knew how to do the same!'

Chapter 4

Miao Shan and Other Legends

Were you with murderous intent
Thrust within a fiery furnace
Lotus Sūtra

Having breathed for a moment the rarified atmosphere of mysticism represented by the Heart Sūtra and descended thence to the lower spurs of Kuan Yin's holy mountain whereon Avalokita and Tara shed their radiance on men and women of ordinary perception, we have still to explore another of the lower peaks where Kuan Yin sits enthroned as a folk goddess worshipped by millions upon millions. These, ignorant of Buddhist metaphysics, love her in the uncomplicated manner of the fisher-folk, recognising in her the protective power and rewarding nature of compassion. Images of her in this aspect are ubiquitous in China (unless swept away by the surge of the Red tide) and neighbouring countries. Smilingly, she gazes on the world from behind the altars of Taoist temples and hermitages, to say nothing of tens of thousands of wayside shrines and grottoes, or of the innumerable dwellings in which some quiet corner is set aside for this most beloved of all divinities. In these days, one finds in Korea and Japan gigantic statues of her so placed as to be visible from afar that people may call to mind, amidst the pitiless struggle for material gain, the beauty of compassion; but I wonder if Kuan Yin welcomes a kind of publicity so reminiscent of cinema billboards and sexy advertisements for toothpaste or bikinis? Her presence is felt more strongly in those little images of clay one comes upon ensconced in some dim and cool recess hard by a miniature waterfall in a garden rockery.

Rocks, willows, lotus pools or running water are often indications of her presence. In the chime of bronze or jade, the sough of wind in the pines, the prattle and tinkle of streams, her voice is heard. The freshness of dew-spangled lotus leaves or the perfume of a single stick of fine incense recalls her fragrance. Not for her the gaudy splendour of the red-faced War God, the magnificent panoply surrounding the Jade Emperor or the selfish luxury of the Western Royal Mother who once fed upon the vital essence of a thousand youths. Even Chang Ô, chaste Goddess of the Moon, is too fastidious in her cold virginity to be congenial to Kuan Yin. Alone among ten thousand gods, Kuan Yin is warm in her compassion, refined in her simplicity. If she is sometimes decked in golden ornaments, it is only because they are employed as a special symbol for denoting celestial Bodhisattvahood.

As a folk-deity, Kuan Yin embodies in herself, besides Avalokita and Tara, the legendary being, Miao Shan. The following legend, though it makes no mention of Miao Shan by name, may be the prototype of the tales concerning that princess. Were one so un-Chinese in spirit as to cavil that it relates to quite a different person, the answer would be a tolerant smile accompanied by some such words as: 'Kuan Yin manifests herself in countless forms to succour sentient beings. Why should not the lady in this story be one of them, Miao Shan another?'

It is not recorded in which reign the following events took place. Many centuries ago, the governor of a certain province, having no sons, felt a specially deep attachment towards his only daughter. Nevertheless, being a proud and irascible official and a staunch upholder of the Confucian virtues, he kept her under firm restraint, so that she rarely had opportunities to glimpse the great world beyond the walls of the gubernatorial mansion. Often she would sit beside the peach-shaped window of her chamber gazing at a nearby hill where stood a stately monastery, wondering what sort of rites and austerities were practised by the saintly inmates. There seemed to be some sort of mystery about the place, for no sooner did she mention it than someone would be sure to switch abruptly to another subject, leaving her words hanging in mid-air. Though normally such rudeness to the daughter of a governor would be unthinkable, she had to put up with it time and time again. Her curiosity mounted until it could be borne no longer. Certain that her father could never be persuaded to allow her to visit the monastery, she decided to go there on her own, though the mere thought of the impropriety of her walking unattended beyond the walls of the women's courtyards was enough to make her blush. Though modest to the point of shyness, she possessed much of her father's determination and strength of will.

Early one morning, when her attendants were breakfasting in an adjoining chamber, she slipped out lightly disguised and left the family compound by a gate rarely watched, it being adjacent to the servants' privy and used only for carrying away its contents to manure the fields. Hurrying across the pastureland, she set off up the hill. A stone-flagged path brought her to a tall gatehouse where the gateman, perceiving that a rich young lady had come to offer incense to the gods and might be prevailed upon to offer gold besides, welcomed her courteously and straightway led her to the great shrine-hall. Overwhelmed by the magnificence of the statues of the Three Pure Ones – the central trinity of Taoist deities – and charmed by the sacred song now flooding the richly appointed hall, she congratulated herself in having come upon a community of saintly men.

Little did she know that saints in that monastery were few, that the greater part of the recluses were fonder of swordplay by day and the art of 'bedroom warfare' by night than of serving the gods they worshipped. In her ignorance she thought it no harm to wander about the public rooms, visiting the many shrines and garden pavilions which were connected one to another by narrow corridors of lacquered woodwork wherein daylight filtered dimly through the papered windows. In one such corridor, she had to pass a group of three or four grey-robed recluses who, seeming to make way, suddenly surrounded her and pushed her roughly into a darkened chamber, her screams being drowned by the clash of ceremonial cymbals coming from a hall nearby.

By this time, the governor, being apprised of his daughter's disappearance, had sent his servants scurrying in all directions; but it was not until shortly before dusk that information was received to the effect that a richly garbed young woman had been seen early in the morning walking up the hill towards the monastery. The mounted servants whom he now despatched to escort her home presently returned without her, saying that the young lady had certainly been at the monastery earlier in the day but was apparently there no longer. Night fell. By now the governor was in a fury. Not stopping to ponder the likelihood of his daughter's being held at the monastery against her will, he had made up his mind that a girl so abandoned as to venture unattended into a place which had long been known for hermits of evil repute was capable of any vileness. No doubt she was at that very moment lying in the arms of some lusty paramour. There could, he thought tempestuously, be only one way of expunging such dire disgrace. Posting a hundred archers round the monastery with orders to slay whatever living creatures ventured forth he sent his soldiers in with lighted torches to burn that den of evil to the ground. Since no one could escape, the guilty child and her paramour must surely suffer the fate they so richly deserved. As the buildings, except for their foundations and tiled roofs, were constructed of lacquered wood, they were an easy prey to the hungry flames. Not a man – or a woman – escaped the fire within and rain of arrows without!

Hiding the hurt to his pride and whatever regret he felt for the fate of his once beloved daughter, the governor, as was his wont, spent the hour after dawn strolling in his private garden to enjoy the early-morning freshness of the flowers. Suddenly the likeness of the dead child materialised before his eyes and the apparition spoke these words: 'Father, though you had no pity on an innocent girl who barely escaped being violated against her will, I cannot help being sad for you, childless as you must now remain. Therefore I have come to bring you some comfort. Know then that Heaven, which often seems as pitiless as you, was moved by my undeserved suffering. As the flames advanced, I was enveloped in a rainbow and wafted above the clouds to the abodes of gods and immortals. There, by way of compensation for my cruel fate, I was promoted to the rank of goddess. It will be my task to comfort the afflicted and rescue those in peril – a task I am peculiarly qualified to perform having so recently plumbed the depths of fear and suffering. Henceforth I shall be known as Kuan Shih Yin, Hearer-of-the-Cries-of-the-World.'

Among the many versions of the Miao Shan legend (which may have been inspired by the tale of the governor's daughter) the following is typical:

In the eleventh year of the Chin T'ien epoch (around 2590 BC), there was a king who, on account of demerits stemming from a former life, was denied the blessing of a son. Accordingly he sought husbands of rare accomplishment and fine presence for his three daughters, hoping to breed outstanding grandsons, the best of whom would be well suited to inherit his kingdom. His youngest daughter, however, rejected all talk of marriage and, on reaching puberty, begged permission to reside at the White Sparrow Convent, there to engage in a life of pious contemplation. 'Agreed!' laughed the king, thinking that this gently nurtured girl would soon long for deliverance from harsh monastic austerities and could then be given the choice of remaining where she was or marrying some well-chosen prince. Alas, the austere life suited her all too well and the king, his patience at an end, embarked upon a series of measures marked by increasing severity to bend her to his will. Rage mounting day by day, he finally had her dragged from the convent and imprisoned in a tower, there to be nourished on unspeakably revolting food. In vain! Drinking to drown his chagrin served only to increase it, until one day he shouted to his henchmen: 'A monstrous child so lost to filial propriety as to deny her father his dearest wish pollutes all under Heaven. The earth must be cleansed of this foul example of disobedience to loving parents, lest the fashion spread and corrupt future generations. See to it this night!'

Sorrowfully his attendants led the little princess to a lonely spot where the headsman awaited her, weeping but not to be deflected from his duty. The child was made to kneel and the headsman, grasping with both hands the terrible sword that had drunk the blood of many a brutal criminal, was preparing to strike when a blinding tempest arose. In a moment the stars were blotted out, thunder roared and a dazzling ray from Heaven shone down upon the kneeling victim. Ere the headsman could regain his courage, a gigantic tiger bounded from the darkness and carried the swooning girl into the nearby hills.

In all the world no tiger of that size existed; the trembling party of executioners swore to the king that this supernaturally proportioned beast was no other than the tutelary god of that region, who had been known on more than one occasion to assume that dread feline form.

From a cavern in the hills, whither the deity had borne her, the Princess Miao Shan now descended into hell and there, by the power of her unsullied purity, compelled its ruler to release every one of the shivering wretches delivered to him for punishment in requital of their evil deeds. Yen Lo Wang, as that deity is called, was aware of his duty to place the inexorable claims of justice before any natural inclination to mercy and, as many have discovered, was not to be deflected from that duty unless by a bribe of quite extraordinary proportions; but who could forbear the sweet pleading of a princess who valued purity more than life itself?

Returning to the dwelling of the tutelary deity, Miao Shan received the signal honour of a visit from Amitābha Buddha in person! Assuming the splendidly shining form known as the Buddha-Body of Reward, he abjured her to seek safety on sea-girt Potala, known to mariners as the Island of P'u-t'o. 'Around that isle, dear child, lies a dragon-haunted ocean into which none but the pure in heart, least of all your father, dare set sail. There you will be able to devote both day and night to blissful meditation and thus at last attain your pious wish to become a Bodhisattva empowered to succour errant beings. Take now this miraculous peach from the garden of Heaven. Besides preserving you from hunger and thirst for one full year, it will ultimately ensure your eternal felicity.' So saying, the Buddha withdrew.

An island deity, summoned from Potala, carried the princess to her new abode, travelling more swiftly than the wind. For nine full years Miao Shan, when not engaged in meditation, performed deeds of compassion which, crowning the merits acquired in previous lives, completed all that remained to enable her to attain the status of Bodhisattvahood. It was at this time that the charming youth Shan Ts'ai (Virtuous Talent) became her acolyte. Thereafter, by virtue of her Bodhisattva's all-seeing eye, she beheld one day a calamity that suddenly befell the third son of the Dragon King of the Eastern Sea.

Wandering the ocean joyously in the form of a fish, he had been caught by a fisherman and was being carried to the market in a pail heavy with the living victims of that day's catch. Instantly Shan Ts'ai was despatched to purchase those unhappy creatures and return them to the sea. His Majesty the Dragon King, apprised by his son of his deliverance, sent Miao Shan a lustrous jewel known as the Night Brilliance Pearl, by the light of which the Bodhisattva would be able to read sacred books to her heart's content, no matter how dark the night. The gift was carried by his own grand-daughter, Lung Nü (Dragon Maiden), who was so entranced by the virtue and loveliness of her uncle's deliverer that she vowed there and then to dedicate her life to the achievement of Bodhisattvahood. To this end, she entered Kuan Yin's service and has ever since been seen in her company.

Some years later, the Princess Miao Shan, divesting herself of her Bodhisattva's glory, returned to her own country for a space and there converted both her father and her mother, enrolling them as disciples of the Buddha.

Thus the story ends.

Another version of the legend speaks of the princess not as Miao Shan but Miao Chên, the daughter of a ruler during the Chou dynasty (1122 to 255 BC). The earlier events are much the same, but in this case the headsman is foiled by the miraculous shattering of his sword. The irascible king is doubly punished, being strangled by a demon and then carried down to hell, whither his daughter follows him and is overcome by the grisly nature of his torments. Finding Yen Lo Wang adamant about the necessity of the sentence being carried out in full, she prays to Amitābha from the depths of her pure heart. Instantly hell's loathsome caverns are transformed by a shower of celestial lotus flowers into a beauteous realm where the spirits of those sentenced to punishment may live in joyous ease. Whereupon Yen Lo Wang, sadly put out by such interference with the course of justice, implores the princess to return forthwith to the upper world, first releasing her father as evidence of his good will. A celestial vehicle shaped like a lotus awaits her at hell's gates and carries her more swiftly than the wind to Potala Island. There she reigns as the Bodhisattva Kuan Yin, devoting herself to the rescue of suffering sentient beings.

In some other legends Kuan Yin, losing most traces of her Buddhist origin, is identified with another and very different deity, Niang Niang, the Heavenly Mother of the Taoist pantheon. Unable to recollect any of the earlier stories of this kind, I offer a relatively modern one, perhaps not more than two hundred years old, since there is internal evidence relating it to the Ch'ing dynasty. It may be thought an unsatisfactory example, but, to my mind, there is no doubt that this story belongs to the Miao Shan cycle. In many versions of the Miao Shan legend, the episode of her escape from the executioner's sword is replaced by an account of how her father orders the destruction by fire of the tower wherein she is confined, but the victim escapes the flames by soaring above them in the form of a graceful white bird. The late origin of the story that follows makes it all the more interesting, for it indicates that in the popular mind, Kuan Yin continues to undergo incarnations replete with Miao Shan-like episodes. I relate it at some length as the details are still fresh in my mind and it possesses much of the charm characteristic of the whole Miao Shan cycle.

At one time there resided in the city of Ch'ang-sha-fu a promising young scholar by the name of Kuo Hsiang-Hsi, a youth well-versed in the Four Books, Five Classics and the art of composing an eight-legged essay. However, his stock of demerits accumulated in former lives was formidable enough to hinder him on two occasions from obtaining his *hsiu-ts'ai* degree, leaving him unqualified for an official appointment that would have brought honour to his family and supported him comfortably for the whole of his working life. Covered with shame, he bore his father's strictures as best he could and made up his mind that, in one way or another, he would carry out his filial obligations to the full. One day a letter arrived summoning him to appear before his uncle, elder brother to his father and a high official in the provincial administration.

'Well, nephew,' exclaimed Commissioner Kuo when the young man hurried round to make his obeisance, 'you have certainly been prompt. Let us go to my library and talk for a while.'

The uncle led him to a wide pearwood couch furnished with a tray of exceptionally elegant opium utensils. Gesturing to his nephew to make himself comfortable, he lay back against the cushions and set to work cooking a small ball of opium over a filigree lamp with a silver needle. When the pipe was ready, he handed it to the youth who, in some embarrassment, exclaimed: 'No, Uncle, thank you, no. I fear I have no head for opium or wine.'

'Better and better,' cried the uncle delightedly. 'I perceive you are just the kind of level-headed youth I had hoped for.' Putting the pipe to his own lips, he added jovially: 'Virtue in the young is much to be desired, but in all things the sage avoids extremes. I hope you will not refuse a little treat I have arranged for you tonight. Barely sixteen, she is the latest and most succulent acquisition of a certain Mother Ma, an agent of the House of Perpetual Spring – breasts like ripe peaches (I mean the girl's, not Mother Ma's), golden-lotus feet unbelievably tiny, moth eyebrows, willow waist. In short, perfection.'

'Thank you indeed, Uncle,' murmured Hsiang-Hsi, blushing from chin to eyebrows. 'I – well, as you know, Uncle, I recently wedded the third daughter of the Wang family and I – I –'

'Spare your blushes, my dear boy. I understand perfectly and was but testing you. Now I am sure you are exactly the right person to undertake an important mission of great delicacy. It is a task that demands just such innate virtue as yours. Without it, that little minx, your newest aunt, would surely get around you with her wiles.'

Puffing forth what some poet once called 'scented clouds of sweet oblivion', Commissioner Kuo explained that his fifth concubine, who at sixteen was old enough to behave with some decorum, had vanished less than an hour before she was due to arrive at his residence and commence her marital duties. Almost as bad, some of his bridal presents had vanished with her. Instead of welcoming his generosity in saving her, a poor scholar's daughter, from abject poverty and placing every luxury and elegance within her reach, she had reportedly eloped with a penniless young man, a scapegrace called Wu who resided near her father's house. It was said they had run off to the slopes of Nan Yeo, an important sacred mountain, and set up house in a disused shrine near its foot. Naturally they could be arrested and punished as the enormity of their crime demanded, but Commissioner Kuo had a benevolent wish to hush the matter up, provided the girl returned to him and

promised to behave with the decorum expected of the minor
wife of an important official.

'So you see, nephew, I have sent for you, tested you and
found you exactly the right sort of person to undertake this delicate commission. As a close relative, you can be depended upon
to observe the discretion essential to our family's reputation.
You are empowered to offer her seducer a sum of money payable
the day he leaves for some distant province of his choice. Who
knows, I might even write to the authorities there and procure
him some sort of employment. Should he prove obstinate, I
shall count upon you to despatch him to the realm of ghosts
with as little fuss as possible and, above all, without your new
auntie's knowledge. It would be disagreeable to have her shed-
ding tears or harbouring something of a grudge against her
loving husband. Such unseemly behaviour would disturb the
tranquillity of what you will observe to be an unusually
harmonious household.'

With these instructions, information pertaining to the route,
a purse of money and a pair of fine horses – one of them
equipped with a leading rein, Hsiang-Hsi was despatched to
do his uncle's bidding, though not without intense reluctance.
His sympathies lay with the hapless girl and he would sooner
have sent his uncle down to the world of ghosts than deprive
the poor child of her lover. It revolted him to think of a sixteen-
year-old girl being forced to bear children to a man who might
well be a good deal older than her grandfather. On the other
hand, he owed to his father's elder brother and head of the entire
clan a filial duty scarcely less absolute than if the hateful old
man had been his father. Having failed to bring honour to the
family by passing his examination, he must on no account act
in a way that might cause an estrangement between his father
and far too powerful uncle. Moreover, according to the Confucian principles by which he himself set great store, the girl
was much at fault. If women were allowed to choose their own
husbands, civilisation would inevitably perish! Persuaded by
these stern and honourable reflections, he hardened his heart
and resolved to carry out every detail of his uncle's instructions,
short of murder.

The journey to Mount Nan Yeo took several days; riding
one horse and leading another is not the swiftest mode of pro-

gress along an unevenly flagged road. It was evening when he reached the foot of the great mountain; its temple-dotted slopes and cloud-piercing peaks were lost in mist. Though the abandoned shrine where he expected to find the errant pair was not far off, it would not do to come upon them locked in each other's embrace; indeed, it would be best if he were to arrive at a time when only the girl was likely to be at home. Thus reflecting and looking around for a sheltered place to pass the night, he came upon a small temple dedicated to the goddess Niang Niang. Going in to investigate, he found to the left of the courtyard a cell equipped with a wooden sleeping-platform, straw-stuffed bedding grey from long use and some primitive cooking utensils. However, long after night had fallen there was no sign of the owner so, having seen to the horses tethered in the courtyard and supped off some cold meat dumplings carried in his saddlebag, he threw himself down to sleep.

He awoke abruptly from what must surely have been a dream. Very clearly he remembered getting up to trace the source of a beam of brilliant light streaming through cracks in the ill-fitting door. His exploration had led him to the shrine-room where, in place of the shabby, crumbling image, he had beheld a gloriously apparelled lady whose head and body emitted rays of shining light. Even the words she had spoken remained vividly in his mind:

'Waste no time on ceremony. Only listen and obey. Know that, times without number century after century, I have appeared among men, sometimes as now with a celestial body composed of light, sometimes as a human being and more than once as a noble horse. Often I have been manifest in a number of guises simultaneously in several of the innumerable world-systems. Known by many names, among them Niang Niang and Kuan Yin, I have often suffered mutilation sooner than accept impious embraces; for, as far back as the middle era of a previous world-system, I vowed myself to chastity lest my power to mitigate suffering be impaired. If that deluded being, your uncle, has his way, my vow will come to nought and with it will be shattered my power to save an ocean-like number of beings as yet unborn. Therefore have I chosen you as the instrument to accomplish my purpose smoothly.'

'What a beautiful dream!' Hsiang-Hsi reflected. 'I wish I

could recall the ending. Naturally it can be attributed to my
bad conscience about that poor girl. Even so, I am bound to
perform my filial duty. But was it truly just a dream? Even now
I can detect something of the fragrance of the goddess as though
her perfume still clung to my robe.' As these thoughts passed
through his mind, the exquisite fragrance seemed to grow
stronger and he hurried to the shrine-room hoping for evidence
that it had been more than a dream. However, nothing was to
be seen besides the decaying statue fronted by a rickety altar.
Presently he fell asleep again, to awake at dawn with the conviction that he had been foolish to confuse the dream-world
with reality.

For all that, he set out on the last lap of his distasteful journey in a chastened mood. The dream had accorded too well
with his private thoughts to allow him to proceed with an untroubled conscience to carry out his family obligation. Two
hours later, he rode into the small grove where stood the abandoned shrine of which his uncle's informant had spoken.
Though the shrine itself was small, there was a shed attached
to it which doubtless afforded the errant couple shelter. There
was no need to investigate; for, seated on the door-sill,
was a simply dressed but very beautiful young lady who
was eyeing him in some alarm. Of her paramour there was
no sign.

Reining in at a suitable distance and dismounting slowly so
as not to increase her alarm, he exclaimed: 'Fifth Lady, I am
happy to make your acquaintance. This insignificant person is
named Kuo Hsiang-Hsi and is your worthless nephew by marriage. Uncle has sent me to escort you safely home. Be sure
you will be welcomed as though no trifling delay in celebrating
your nuptials had occurred.' Seeing her flush, he added gently:
'Please cause no difficulty. If you do, someone dear to you will
suffer.' So saying, he allowed his glance to travel to the sword
hanging from his saddle.

'There is no one dear to me in this vicinity,' she answered
coldly, 'unless you propose to slaughter the chaste and holy
nuns in the convent higher up this path. Be sure they are blameless. Sooner than bring your uncle's wrath upon them, I have
decided to stay here on my own until the matter has passed from
his mind. If, on the other hand, you refer to the generous young

man who risked his life to escort me here, you will look for him in vain. He knew of my wish for a peaceful convent life too well to linger here once his task was done. It is not in your power to do him harm. As for me, I shall die sooner than surrender myself to that lust-deluded old man. If he desires my corpse, you must arrange things as you think best.'

Lest she do herself an injury forthwith, Hsiang-Hsi leapt towards her and, with as much gentleness as the circumstances permitted, drew her on to his second horse, where he secured her person to the saddle in a way so cunning that no one would detect the silken cords masked by the folds of her garments. Thus she need not endure the shame of being recognised as his captive, nor he submit to being questioned by officers or ordinary travellers they might encounter on the road.

'Best not call for help, Fifth Lady. I have a warrant for your arrest issued by Commissioner Kuo and a document stamped with his seal authorising me to effect it. No one who sees them will dare render you assistance. The chief result would be to involve yourself and my uncle in unnecessary shame.'

'Virtuous little lily-faced scholar,' was her swift retort. 'Think well what you are doing. My death might not burden your conscience, but it would provide you with a load of evil karma with effects reaching through many lives to come.'

Mounting his horse, to which the leading rein of hers was firmly fastened, he replied: 'Whatever the cost, Fifth Lady, I must perform my filial duty. If you struggle with your bonds, I shall be compelled to mount you on the crupper of my saddle – an undignified way of travelling you would greatly dislike.' Urging the horses to a trot, he set out on the homeward path.

When they reached the wayside temple where he had passed the night, she begged so prettily to be allowed to enter and pay her respects to the goddess that he could not well refuse, though determined not to let her out of his sight. However, while his hands were busy tethering the horses, she slipped into the shrine-room; running after her, he saw a sight that made him fall to his knees and touch his head to the floor, all thought of responsibility forgotten. The decaying statue had vanished, as in his dream, but this time to be replaced by none other than the Fifth Lady herself. Encircled by a glowing nimbus, she reclined upon a vividly coloured lotus throne, flanked by two shining spirits – the easily recognised Shan Ts'ai and the Dragon Girl, Lung Nü!

'Homage to the Greatly Compassionate, Greatly Merciful Kuan Shih Yin Bodhisattva Mahasattva!' gabbled the terrified young scholar, repeating it many times for good measure and hoping that the honorific 'Mahasattva' might dispose her to pardon him more readily.

'Oh cease your muttering and pay attention,' cried the Bodhisattva, in the very tones of the Fifth Lady whom she so perfectly resembled. 'Not altogether unmoved by your simple-minded notion of filial piety, We have been pleased to manifest Ourself to you in this holy place to save you from a grievous error that would otherwise hang like a stone about your neck for many lifetimes yet to come. Having beheld Us thus with waking eyes, it is not fitting that you return to the world of dust. Not for you its lusts, its hatreds and its follies. Either you will take Us back to the shrine whence We were so rudely abducted and, proceeding thence to the Lotus Calyx Monastery, there take monastic vows and live until this life is past; or else I shall return to Ch'ang-sha-fu as your captive and let the events that will come to pass take their predetermined course – for you, a sad one.'

Most eagerly Hsiang-Hsi agreed to do her bidding, all stuffy notions of filial piety now fled. In a flash the effects of twenty years of Confucian training had been dissipated by the power of this radiant being.

The Bodhisattva, withdrawing in some mysterious way from the body of the Fifth Lady, who again became an ordinary human being, now vanished. Hsiang-Hsi escorted his 'aunt' back to her shrine and himself continued up the path to seek admission to the monastery. This was accorded readily and in the course of time he was ordained.

Meanwhile Commissioner Kuo, fearing his nephew had been murdered or abducted, rode at the head of a troop of soldiers as fast as their horses would carry them to Nan Yeo. Finding the wayside shrine deserted and learning from some local peasants that the beautiful lady had recently removed to the Convent of Sweet Dew, he furiously ordered his men to follow him up the mountain. Investing the nunnery from all sides, they fired its sacred buildings; and as the terrified nuns, driven back into the inferno by a rain of arrows, crowded piteously beneath an archway that afforded a momentary respite, Commissioner Kuo gazed triumphantly at the face of the girl who had eluded his lusts only to suffer a cruel death. But, when the flames had burnt out and the soldiers had collected the charred remains of the victims, though all the eleven nuns were accounted for, no trace of the Fifth Lady could be discovered. This circumstance so added to the Commissioner's rage that a fierce heat mounted to his head, causing him to fall upon the ground and there expire. His final agony passed unnoticed by his followers, whose eyes were fixed upon a beautiful white bird that flew round the monastery three times before ascending and, flying ever higher, vanished beyond the gold and crimson gates of heaven. Nor was that the only marvel they beheld, for the consciousness-components of the slaughtered nuns, rising from their pitiful remains, ascended heavenwards in the wake of that soaring bird!

So ends the story – obviously a version of the Miao Shan story brought relatively up to date. What is not absolutely clear is whether the Fifth Lady, besides being possessed in the shrine-room by the goddess, was or was not an actual incarnation of Kuan Yin. The monk from whom I heard the story did not know.

A slighter and more trivial story, related to me by a young novice vowed as a thank-offering to the monastery while still a child, brings Miao Shan right into the twentieth century, that is if those who beheld the apparition of Kuan Yin were right in supposing that the exceptionally youthful form she assumed was that of Miao Shan. In some ways the tale is closer to those related of the youthful Tara than to the Miao Shan cycle; for which reason I had some hesitation in placing it in its present context.

'My parents', declared the novice, 'vowed me to the service of the Buddha at the time of Elder Brother's illness. He was lying at the point of death, you see, when Kuan Yin's mercy saved him. When the physician told us there was no hope, my aunt shooed him from the house and took over. Calling all the neighbours in, she ordered them to spend the night in our house, reciting the Dhāranī of Great Compassion until dawn. The harvest had been brought in safely, otherwise they might have been less docile, though my aunt is not a person one cares to cross. Towards midnight Elder Brother, who had been lying all day in a coma, startled us by raising his head and shouting weakly: "Look at that girl!" His eyes were fixed upon the rafters where, to our great astonishment, sat a fairy-like girl in long antique robes. (Several people said later that she was the very image of those pictures of Miao Shan one sees in those old-fashioned cartoon books which still follow the style of the Ch'ing dynasty. That meant nothing to me, for I had not seen the cartoons or ever heard of Miao Shan, but that is what they said.) I would not say that the girl's form was very clear, only that it was too clear for anyone to suppose it to be a trick of light and shadow. Besides, she was laughing and we all heard that. In her hands was a kind of vase like the one in which Kuan Yin stores the dew of compassion, as it is called. She was playing with it like a prankish child and suddenly tipped it sharply so that some liquid fell right on my brother's head. Then she was gone and everybody burst out talking at once. What a noise! My aunt was jubilant. After taking a good look at my brother, she said there was no need to go on with what she called the cure, meaning the mantra recitation. Within a couple of days, Elder Brother was on his feet. The physician was speechless when, within less than a week, Elder Brother walked over to the neighbouring village to offer him a basket of fruit! Oh, I forgot. It was when they began to recite the mantra that my aunt persuaded my parents to vow me to the monastery as a thank-offering for their eldest son's recovery. I am glad they did. I like it here.'

As Kuan Yin, under the name Kwannon-sama, has achieved much the same degree of popularity in Japan as in China, I shall relate one Japanese story that is at once like and yet different from its Chinese counterparts.

The birth of Chūjō Hime, daughter of the noble Fujiwara Toyonari (eighth century AD) unfortunately cost her mother's life. (Her mother, by the way, is reputed to have been an incarnation of Kwannon-sama.) The girl was distinguished throughout her childhood for her lively pity for people and animals in distress, yet her step-mother ill-treated her with relentless cruelty, even going so far as to make attempts upon her life! Poor Chūjō Hime fled to Mount Hibari in the province

1 Characteristic painting of Kuan Yin voyaging upon a giant lotus petal (Modern. Author's collection)
2 Wooden image of Kuan Yin from a South China fisherman's junk (Recent. Courtesy of Mr K. E. Stevens)
3 Statue of Kuan Yin, right hand raised in blessing, from Yunnan Province, South-West China (13th c. Courtesy of the British Museum)

2

4 Exceedingly fine Chinese gilded wooden statue of Avalokita, Kuan Yin's main Indian progenitor, almost half life-size (13th c. Courtesy of Mr David Kidd and Mr Yasuyoshi Morimoto, whose Japanese palace it long adorned)

5 Nepalese bronze statue of Tara, Kuan Yin's second Indian progenitor, who is generally depicted in a sitting posture (11–12th c. Courtesy of the British Museum)

6 Painting of the Thousand-Armed Avalokita from the Tun Huang
caves, showing strong Indo-Tibetan influence (*c.* 7th c. Courtesy of
the British Museum)

7 Magnificent Mongolian gilded bronze image of Tara from the Palace Museum in the Republic of Mongolia (17th c. Courtesy of Mr Wongchindorj)

8a Porcelain image of Kuan Yin as a Giver of Offspring
b Wooden image from Amoy, South China, of Shan Ts'ai, Kuan Yin's male attendant
c Wooden image from Canton, South China, of Lung Nü (the Dragon Maiden), Kuan Yin's female attendant (All recent and from the collection of Mr K. E. Stevens)

7

8a   b   c

9   Statue of Kuan Yin holding the vase of
'sweet dew' and the wish-fulfilling gem (A.D.
595. Courtesy of the British Museum)

10   Painting of Amitābha Buddha, of whom
Kuan Yin is an emanation, from the Tun
Huang caves (T'ang Dynasty, 6–9th c. Cour-
tesy of the British Museum)

11 Painting of Amitābha Buddha as the Guide of Souls from the Tun Huang caves (Perhaps T'ang Dynasty, 6–9th c. Courtesy of the British Museum)

12 Statue of Kuan Yin holding the vase of 'sweet dew' (Liao Dynasty, 12th c. Courtesy of the British Museum)

13 Statue of Kuan Yin in a very characteristic pose known as 'lordly ease' (12th c. Courtesy of the British Museum)

14 Statue of Kuan Yin holding a fish basket,
symbol of fecundity (date and provenance unknown. Courtesy of Mr K. G. Stevens)

15 Curious statue of Kuan Yin (T'ang Dynasty, 6–9th c. Courtesy of the British Museum)

16 Nepalese bronze statue of Manjuśri, embodiment of Wisdom (A.D. 1819. Courtesy of the British Museum)

of Kii, causing great suffering to her father, who searched two long years before finding her.

'Beloved child,' he exclaimed when their transports of joy had subsided, 'I bring you the best of news. A marriage has been arranged for you – no, do not interrupt – to no less a person than our Tenno, Son of Heaven and Emperor of Japan!'

'Poor Father,' replied Chūjō Hime sorrowfully, 'though you have set your heart on this, it can never be. You must pray His Majesty to excuse me, for I have vowed before the Buddha to remain single all my life, so as to devote my whole time to the attainment of Bodhisattvahood for the benefit of all sentient beings.'

Thereafter, unshaken by her father's anger or his sadness, she entered Taima-deva Convent in the province of Yamato. There she undertook a long series of rigorous austerities, daily beseeching Amidabutzu (Amitābha Buddha) to appear and vouchsafe her an omen of success in the attainment of Bodhisattvahood. Receiving no response, at last she cried: 'Holy Amidabutzu, until you kindly manifest yourself, no food shall pass my lips and you will be responsible for my dying of starvation!'

Thereupon an elderly stranger arrived at her door and, after some converse, promised to show her Amidabutzu's paradise, provided she would accept some unusual instructions from the Mother Superior. Soon afterwards, she was commanded to gather a hundred loads of lotus stalks and carefully separate the fibres. This she did and, still in obedience to the Mother Superior's instructions, placed them in a well which had miraculously appeared in the courtyard. On contact with its pure water, the fibres took on enchanting colours of rainbow-like variety. This marvel accomplished, there now appeared a young woman with a loom who, in the space of a mere six hours, wove an exquisite picture of Amidabutzu's Pure Land, which was all the more miraculous in that the picture was somehow much larger than the room which contained it! Deeply moved, Chūjō Hime bowed her head to the ground before it; whereat, to her intense joy, the elderly stranger and young weaver revealed themselves as Amidabutzu and Kwannon-sama!

One episode in the charming little story – the one where the young girl actually dares to *threaten the Buddha*(!) strikes me as peculiarly Japanese. No Chinese devotee would be so lost to the dictates of propriety!

Chapter 5

Some Buddhist Concepts of Kuan Yin

To the perfection of her merits,
Worshipping, we bow our heads
                    Lotus Sūtra

I have always been intrigued by those masterpieces of Chinese ivory carving comprising a large number of exquisitely carved balls revolving one within another. Being intricately decorated, the outer layers largely conceal those within; though one gazes long and hard, it is not easy to discern the innermost ball or even to distinguish clearly one middle layer from another. So it was with my perception of Kuan Yin, some of her more and less materialistic aspects seeming to be inextricably intertwined. This was especially true of the levels of understanding at which she gradually exchanges her goddess-like attributes for those of a Bodhisattva. The guise she wears for those who burn incense to her in wayside shrines and mountain grottoes or in the temples of the fisher-folk and boat-dwellers undergoes no startling change when she presents herself to the less erudite members of Chinese and Japanese Buddhist communities. True, they know her by her proper title, Bodhisattva, but some would be hard put to it to explain in what manner gods and Bodhisattvas differ. The Mahayana sutras chiefly prized by the Pure Land Sect to which many of her devotees belong do not easily yield their hidden meaning. Indeed, they resemble the profound tantric works revered by Tibetans in that, if taken literally in the absence of oral instruction from a Master, they may repel rather than attract most Western students of the Way, who may deem them too full of marvels to merit serious attention.

Were the approach taken here to understanding Kuan Yin's true significance to be made fully consistent, it would be necessary to set forth the Pure Land teaching and practices as they appear to the uninstructed and reserve their esoteric meaning for a later chapter. However, that is not quite how I came upon them myself; thanks to the guidance of some Chinese friends, I began to have at least a vague conception of the esoteric meaning while still near the outset of my studies and I have ordered my exposition accordingly. Like a fair number of other Western Buddhists, I began by shying away from what could be seen of Pure Land practice all about me in South China, being unable as yet to reconcile it with the Buddhist teaching familiar to me. Though its manifestations were always beautiful, I did not believe they had much relation to reality.

Briefly, the doctrine in its literal form is that the Buddha, foreseeing the onset of a decadent age (in the midst of which we now find ourselves today) and recognising how difficult it would be for the beings born in that age to pursue Enlightenment by the means he had expounded hitherto, compassionately presented a much easier way. He delivered some sutras (discourses) anent celestial Buddhas such as Amitābha and Bodhisattvas such as Kuan Yin, each of whom had mentally created a spiritual realm (Pure Land) wherein all beings who aspired to it earnestly could secure rebirth under conditions ideally suited to making progress towards Enlightenment. Profiting by the vast merits of the creator of their chosen Pure Land, such beings, however great their demerits, could easily attain rebirth in, for example, Kuan Yin's Potala and thus escape the dreary round of birth, suffering and death endlessly renewed which is samsara. Furthermore, those celestial Buddhas and Bodhisattvas were portrayed as wielding miraculous powers wherewith they could instantly avert danger or affliction from any being who called upon them with absolute sincerity; thus, even should one be kneeling beneath an executioner's sword already raised to strike, a single heart-felt cry to Kuan Yin Bodhisattva would cause the blade to fall shattered to the ground!

Well, this teaching, though couched in terms of the utmost beauty, struck me as too good to be true, too redolent of primitive conceptions of heaven and of fairy godmother tales like Cinderella. However, my Chinese friends advised me not to dismiss the teaching out of hand, but rather to seek its inner purport. Soon after my arrival in the East, I had struck up a warm friendship with a most unusual man, a Chinese physician and keen Buddhist about ten years my senior. I was immediately attracted to him for several reasons, not the least of which was his fondness for tradition as exemplified by his garb – instead of a Western-style business suit, a mode of dress already becoming common in Hong Kong, he wore a graceful silken robe surmounted by an old-fashioned skull-cap of stiff black satin with a tiny scarlet bobble at the crown. Being fond of the more esoteric forms of Buddhism, he had first mastered the Shingon form recently brought back to China from Japan and then embarked on a life-long study of the Vajrayana taught by Tibetan lamas; and, with regard to the Pure Land Sect and others, he retained the typically Chinese attitude which the Venerable T'ai Hsü once summed up in the words: 'All the sects are like beads on one rosary.' It was to Ta Hai, my physician friend, that I took some doubts about the Pure Land teaching which persisted despite my feeling a special affinity to Kuan Yin.

'Elder Brother, since having that odd experience, I have been thinking much about Kuan Yin,' I said one day, handing him an opened copy of the Heart of Great Compassion Dhāraṇī Sūtra and pointing to the words: '*Should any being recite and cleave to the sacred Dhāraṇī of Great Compassion and yet not be reborn in my Buddhaland, I vow not to enter upon Supreme Enlightenment.*'

'As you know', I continued, 'there are many passages in the sutras which state that one who calls upon her name with great sincerity or recites her mantra from his heart will surely be reborn in her sacred Potala and there be trained to achieve Enlightenment. Does that not strike you as too easy to be true? Elsewhere the sutras stress again and again that the seed of Enlightenment latent in every being must be watered by self-cultivation, that no teacher, human or divine, can do the work on our behalf. Granted that those descriptions of Pure Lands full of jewelled trees, gem-studded lotus pools and birds warbling the sacred teaching can be understood figuratively and putting aside the fact that such descriptions come oddly from the lips of people who share our belief in the Mind Only doctrine, there is another obstacle. How can you reconcile the need for self-power (*tzû-li*) with the Pure Land Sect's reliance on other-power (*t'a-li*)? It seems so very illogical.'

Ta Hai laughed delightedly. 'I think, Ah Jon, you are still foreign-devil-man and cannot learn to think like Chinese. Why you care about logical, not logical? Truth have plenty faces. As you see things, so things are. As you expect things, so things come. Why? Because your mind make them so. You dream long time of jewelled paradise, you surely take rebirth there. You think wisdom help you reach formless world, you surely take rebirth there. You have learnt to recite Heart Sūtra, yes? So you know very well "Form is void and void is form; form not differ from void, void not differ from form." Then why you worry these nonsense things? I and my friends tell you and tell you and tell you that appearances are all in mind. Why you not understand? Outside mind – nothing!'

'Yes, but –'

'Listen, Ah Jon. Pure Land teacher say fix mind on sacred name or speak sacred mantra many, many times, then your mind become still, yes? All obscurations disappear. That way, you know, plenty people get objectless awareness which is first step to Enlightenment. That is very good, no? So why you care *how* they get it? All of us Buddhists are looking for goal higher than man can see or imagine. You agree? Good. Suppose my picture of goal is dull and your picture seems to you much clearer, you know quite well that both those pictures must be a long, long way – a million miles and more – from truth picture. We go one million mile walk; you start one inch in front of me not help you much, Ah Jon. Your talk about *tzû-li* and *t'a-li* sound very good, very clever, very wise to you? To me, all nonsense! You want to study Buddha Dharma, you must study mind. Only mind is real, but now you try to put front door and back door on it! Self? Other? Inside? Outside? How can be? Some people look for Enlightenment in mind. Some people look for Bodhisattva. You find them different? Never can be! Why? Because whole universe live inside your bony skull. Nowhere else at all. Amitābha Buddha in your skull. Kuan Yin Bodhisattva in your skull. Ch'an (Zen) followers seek Enlightenment from mind. Pure Land followers seek it in Pure

Land. What difference? Two thoughts; one Source. You are philosopher, so think one way. Your friend just love Kuan Yin, so think another. Different, yes! What difference? Two faint ideas, same shining truth.

'You seek stirring of compassion in mind, soon you find. Seek shining compassion-being like Kuan Yin, soon you find. Suppose you run out in street now, tell everybody must use self-power, not other-power; you think they understand? Or they stand there gaping? You ought to welcome compassionate Buddha's thousand ways of teaching thousand kinds of people.'

I believe I learned more from Ta Hai than from any other man, but it was not all plain sailing. His English was worse than I have represented it here and my Cantonese no better at that time. We managed to tackle all kinds of abstruse subjects, helping out the words with gestures, drawings and Chinese written characters, but relying greatly on the kind of telepathic understanding by which close friends can surmount most language barriers. With others of our group it was often easier, as some spoke English very well indeed. Asked why many Pure Land followers seemed to prefer evoking Kuan Yin rather than Amitābha Buddha of whom she is but an emanation, one of them replied:

'Like you, they feel drawn to her. It is because of your nature. If you were a horse, you would be sure to invoke the Horse-Headed Hayagrīva, who is also Kuan Yin. If a lobster, you would choose a lobster deity, just as nagas invoke serpent divinities. Picturing compassion in the form of a lovely woman is a reasonable thing to do. Amitābha Buddha is compassion seen as a noble quality, shining and majestic; Kuan Yin is compassion seen as intimate and a counterpart of gentle pity. Not having many heads in the Indian manner nor necessarily sharing Amitābha's vastness, she appeals to humanists like you and me and fits in well with our Chinese conception of divinity.'

From all of this I began drawing a conclusion that proved absolutely wrong, for when I voiced it they opposed it vehemently and I perceived that the waters we had entered were deeper than they seemed.

'Do you mean', I asked, 'that Amitābha, Kuan Yin and their vows to succour sentient beings are really myths used to persuade unlearned people to concentrate upon their names and thus achieve one-pointedness of mind even though unable to perceive its proper purpose?'

Before the words were well out of my mouth, I realised I had uttered an enormity. They glanced at one another in consternation – not, I think, because like Jovians in a similar situation they expected a shower of thunderbolts to greet this blasphemy, but because they were aghast that their way of putting things had led me so far astray, or perhaps they were just bewildered by my obtuseness.

'Make no mistake,' cried old Mr Lao sharply, speaking in Cantonese in his eagerness to set the record straight. 'The Buddhas, the Bodhisattvas and their vows are real. It you doubt it, you will be beyond their help!'

'But –'

'Look at this blackwood desk. Is it real, do you think?'

'Yes, of course – real in the limited sense that any phenomenon is real. You can see and touch it.'

'Good. How about, say, justice? We are told, for example, that Britain's legal system ensures you people a greater measure of justice than is to be had in Hong Kong. Is justice real?'

'Ye-es. If you put it that way. Justice can be quantified to some extent and seen to exist in one place but not in another. It would make sense to say that all justice had been banished from such-and-such a country.'

'Excellent. Though you cannot hurt your hand by banging it against justice, you do agree it is real. But *why* is it real? Because mind conceives it. If human beings were mindless entities like motor-cars, there could be no such thing as justice. Whatever the mind conceives thereby achieves reality. Suppose it were found that, after all, our national sage, Confucius, had no historical existence, would it alter the fact of his overwhelming influence on our country? Conceived of in the way he is, he would have become a reality and his reported words and actions, as the causes of great effects, would also have reality. Be sure that Kuan Yin's vow is real, that if you earnestly desire rebirth in her Potala paradise, you will take birth there.'

Such were the conversations Ta Hai and his friends most enjoyed and great was my bewildered admiration of their wisdom. The questions and answers reported above may seem obscure unless one has a background knowledge of Mahayana Buddhism. The crux of the matter is as follows:

According to that teaching, it is not profitable to spend time on such questions as whether there was ever a beginning to the succession of universes that have been arising and reaching their end for innumerable aeons, or why sentient beings must revolve endlessly from life to life in this sad realm of samsara. What is needed is to direct one's attention to the *present*, thinking: 'This is how things are; what is to be done about them?' It is taught that reality has two aspects – the realms of Void and form – but that, due to obscurations arising from primordial ignorance and from evil karma accumulated in past lives, we fail to *see* that nothing can exist independently of everything else, that all entities (including people) are transient, mutable, unsatisfying and *lacking in own-being*. It is the illusion of possessing an ego that leads to such obscurations as passion, lust and inordinate desire. From these in turn spring a longing for continued *individual* existence which keeps beings revolving in the round of birth and death, reaping over and over again sorrow, frustration, disappointment, grief, adversity. Could one but be rid of all ego-born delusions, he would see himself as a shadow pursuing shadows and eagerly seek an end to the round – not in extinction, but in Nirvāna, the glorious apotheosis in which illusory egos are no more. The way out lies within each sentient being's mind in the form of latent wisdom-compassion energy (Bodhi). This is so because so-called individual minds are not truly apart from Mind, the Plenum in which everything exists forever and forever in the form of '*no thing*'. When entities vanish, nothing is lost, for they had no ultimate existence in the first place, being nevertheless real because not divorced from the Void.

Liberation is achieved by Enlightenment, the fruit of transcending all ego-delusion. A powerful technique for attaining it is meditation (better called contemplation) which results in a turning over of the mind upon itself, the expulsion of obscurations and recognition of oneself and all beings as being wholly without self or anything describable as own-being. Thus the effort has to be *self-effort*. No wise guru, no high divinity can accomplish this revolution on one's behalf; it must occur of itself. Now comes the surprise and seeming contradiction.

Adherents of the Pure Land School seek a way out through rebirth in a 'Pure Land' where they can give themselves over to the great task of seeking Enlightenment under ideal conditions, there being no hindrances, but only powerfully favourable influences. Exoterically it is taught that the Buddha Amitābha (like some others such as Kuan Yin) vowed to save all beings who call upon him wholeheartedly by admitting them to a Pure Land, this being his compassionate means of assisting those weak in self-power or too ignorant to understand how to use it. Esoterically it is recognised that the Pure Land is no other than Pure Mind, the condition of all minds when purged of ego-born obscurations. But this distinction between the exoteric and esoteric understanding of the doctrine is not simple or sharp-cut. Even exceedingly erudite Buddhists such as Ta Hai hold that the various Pure Lands, including Kuan Yin's Potala, do in a sense exist as places, since mind has thus conceived them. This seemingly startling departure from logic is somewhat less puzzling if one accepts that *all* entities are mental creations, none ultimately more or less real than any other.

A devotional approach, like that of Pure Land followers, is currently out of favour in the West, being too reminiscent of the Christian and Jewish faiths which many people no longer find acceptable. Few Asians share this antipathy. Even Theravada (southern) Buddhism has a greater element of devotional practice than is generally recognised by Westerners. The same is true of Ch'an (Zen) Buddhism, many of whose most ardent followers (including the great Daisets Suzuki) have affirmed the validity of the Pure Land doctrine and regard Pure Land practices as a particularly efficient means of attaining Enlightenment. Even today, the Pure Land School has a much greater following among Japanese Buddhists than any other, as it had in China prior to the submergence of all religion beneath the waters of the Red flood. Under present circumstances, Pure Land practice may not be well suited to the West; nevertheless, its critics among Western Buddhists would do well to ponder the implications of Mahayana philosophy more deeply before dismissing Pure Land teachings, as they sometimes do, as being contrary to the spirit of traditional Buddhism. As Asian Buddhists have always understood, different kinds of people need to make widely different approaches to the same truth.

This is possible because one is not dealing with *understanding*, which is to some extent governed by the rules of logic, but with a *practice* that, if properly performed, will achieve results however one may initially conceive of it. A man who presses an electric light switch will succeed in turning on the light, even if he happens to be under the impression that he is switching on the radio.

To return to Kuan Yin. I believe my friend's point about invoking the Bodhisattva embodying wisdom-compassion in a form well suited to a people's cultural traditions was a good one; but, in my opinion, there may also be another reason for the preference given to Kuan Yin by people whose beliefs are generally in line with those of the Pure Land School. The visualisation prescribed for meditators in the Amitayus Sūtra is very difficult to perform in comparison with the popular manner of meditating upon Kuan Yin. When engaged in the sutra-type meditation, one has to build up a complicated picture involving, for example, the mental creation of eight pools flowing into fourteen channels, each with the radiant colours of seven jewels; in each pool there are 600,000 lotuses, each with seven jewels and each possessing a girth twelve times the distance covered by an army in a day's march! Amitābha's height equals that same distance multiplied by the number of sand-grains in *sixty thousand million million* rivers each of them the size of the Ganges! It is written that all this, and very much else besides, has to be visualised as clearly as one sees his hand before his eyes! The mind boggles – which is just what is intended, for, as with Ch'an (Zen) koans, the purpose is to exhaust the mind to the point where it is jerked into a new dimension. When successfully performed, this type of visualisation leads to a sudden transformation of consciousness, thereby opening up new realms hitherto far beyond the uttermost bounds of perception. Still, the task *is* daunting. The simple contemplation of Kuan Yin described in the chapter on meditation may perhaps be less effective, but is certainly better suited to the limited competence of ordinary meditators.

This view of the matter was suggested to me by a pamphlet I discovered in the very embryonic library of the school-room for novices in the Hua T'ing Monastery near Kunming. Locally printed, it was the work of a strange-looking man who occasion-

ally paid us visits. Carelessly dressed, much given to laughter
at unexpected moments, he would have impressed me as
slightly demented, but for his reputation for wisdom – a great
many holy men in China's history are reputed to have made
just such an impression of daftness on their more staid contemporaries. Unable to recall more than the general purport
of the pamphlet, I have had to fill in the details from my imagination, but my version is faithful in spirit to the original.

It began with some information regarding the writer's
identity, birth-place, family and so forth, and then proceeded
on the following lines:

'My father and grandfather, Confucian scholars of the old
school, looked on Buddhists with disfavour, believing them to
delude people with lurid tales of magic. It was through my
mother – an unusually highly literate woman from a village near
Ta Li – that I came upon the profound doctrine known as "the
voidness of non-void". Not that she herself had much interest
in such profundities. A devoted follower of the Pure Land
School, she cared nothing for metaphysics, but it was her custom to buy whatever Buddhist works the pedlar who supplied
us happened to bring. As a small child I learned to recite the
sacred formula, Hail to Amitābha Buddha! many hundreds of
times a day, though always in secret for fear of my father's
anger. My mother believed that one-pointed repetition of this
formula was enough in itself to ensure liberation from the round
of birth and death. Once when my classmates in the middle
school heard me softly invoking Amitābha Buddha they jeered
at me so heartily that, to win back their esteem, I took to bringing to school Buddhist works which they had to admit would
tax the understanding of erudite scholars. Pretending I understood these works myself, I came to study them in all serious-
ness. I believed then that the Pure Land practice was suitable
only for women, peasants and similarly ill-educated people, and
had turned instead to such works as The Pure Consciousness
Treatise, the Avatamsaka and Lankāvatāra Sūtras. They
availed me nothing, their only effect being to disturb my mind,
so I returned to invoking Amitābha Buddha, but not without
reflecting smugly that my understanding of this practice
was now at a "higher level" than my mother's! How ignorant I
must have seemed to her! "Higher" and "lower", "deep" and

"shallow", what have these dualisms to do with knowledge, wisdom, understanding?

'Once I went to listen to a lecture on Pure Land contemplation by a famous Tripitaka Master who fired me with ambition to visualise scenes of unimaginable vastness. This, too, got me nowhere. Having painfully built up a huge and glittering background of immense, heavily bejewelled trees and lakes, I had to set about creating images of the Three Holy Ones. No sooner had I started on Amitābha Buddha than the background slipped away; starting on Kuan Yin Bodhisattva, I lost Amitābha; starting on Mahāsthāma Bodhisattva, I lost Kuan Yin. It was all beyond my power. Only conceit hindered me from going back to simple repetition of the sacred formula, which my mother had never for one day abandoned.

'One night I dreamed of being shipwrecked, of clinging to a spar in a furiously raging sea. Mountainous waves curved about me like writhing dragons until, at last, I was cast upon a shore of unearthly beauty. Overlooking the rocky coast, a hill of turquoise rose from a forest of jade that was watered by foaming cascades of milk-white purity. The wings of birds and insects had a jewelled sheen; the spotted deer had coats of white and crimson fur. How could I doubt that I had come upon the sea-girt paradise, Potala? Awed, but joyous, I climbed swiftly towards the crest of the hill.

'I had been observed, for a young girl came running down the slope to greet me. Her charming little feet seemed scarcely to touch the rocks over which she sped. When she turned and signalled me to follow her, I had difficulty in keeping up and was irked to notice how torn she was between good manners and an urge to burst out laughing. On our reaching the mouth of a great turquoise cavern, she ran in and soon disappeared from view, leaving me to follow as best I could. We had come to this place by skirting a lake of gold-flecked blue, an arm of which ran into the cave, its blue water hidden beneath masses of pink and white lotus. Though no direct sunlight penetrated beyond the entrance, the cave was illuminated as though by bright sunshine and a delicate fragrance filled the air. In the centre was a throne-shaped rock. Though it had neither cushions nor occupant, I knew it for the Bodhisattva's own and, kneeling, bowed my head to the gleaming silver sand at its foot.

As I did so, my name was spoken by a voice as melodious as the tinkling of jade ornaments, the syllables distinct and long drawn out.

' "Cheng-Li, when my vow was uttered many aeons ago, I thought I had made things simple. Why do you *strive*? Let go! The whole Mahayana Canon contains no greater wisdom than the wisdom of letting go. This is also called *dāna*, giving."

'There came a sweetly joyous laugh, then silence. I knew I was now alone in that shining cave. Already the magical colours were fading into powder-fine coloured sparks that vanished one by one. Darkness followed and, stretching out my hand, I brushed it against the gauze curtains hung around my bed.

'Now I have done with sutras and pious practices. Day and night I recite the Bodhisattva's sacred name, rejoicing in the beauty of its sound. Not for me its recitation in multiples of a hundred and eight, as though it were a duty. Does the runner count his breaths or the poet his words, or the stream its ripples? You sentient beings who seek deliverance, why do you not – let go? When sad, let go of the cause for sadness. When wrathful, let go of the occasion of wrath. When covetous or lustful, let go of the object of desire. From moment to moment, be free of self. Where no self is, there can be no sorrow, no desire; no I to weep, no I to lust, no "being" to die or be reborn. The winds of circumstance blow across emptiness. Whom can they harm?'

Like many writings of this kind, it concluded with verses conveying the essence of its meaning. I remember that they were beautiful and made much of the magical setting – the gold-flecked lotus pool, the turquoise mountain ringed with a forest of jade leaves and the 'dragon-curving waves'. The Chinese language lends itself to poetic descriptions of this sort and its monosyllabic character saves the verses from being heavy or ornate. The verses went on to epitomise the qualities pertaining to a Bodhi-mind or heart of compassion and, at the end, came some such lines as:

> Wrathful, banish thought of selfhood;
> Sad, let fall the cause of woe;
> Lustful, shed lust's mental object;
> Win all by simply letting go.

However, I am sure the original concluding verse was a great deal more arresting.

Having received little personal instruction from Tripitaka Masters of the Pure Land School, I am not confident of having grasped the profound inner meaning of its teachings. It does not do to conceive of Kuan Yin and her Potala in the materialistic terms acceptable to the unlettered, who fully expect to behold physical splendours when the Bodhisattva, in response to their frequent invocations, comes to succour them at the moment of death; but nor should one treat the Pure Land sutras as wholly allegorical, or suppose that the Pure Land practice is of value only until the devotee 'enters the Potala' in the sense of recognising it to be his own mind purged of obscurations. One must avoid an over-materialistic concept on the one hand and a purely allegorical interpretation on the other. Were you to say that Kuan Yin and her Potala exist objectively, you would be scolded for talking nonsense; but claim that she is wholly a creation of your own mind and you will be taken to task for arrogance or laughingly reminded that the Bodhisattva existed a long time before you were born. Perhaps full understanding is a fruit not to be won without intensive Pure Land practice, for there is certainly no logical solution to the riddle.

A recent exposition of the main practice of the Pure Land Sect – sustained recitation of one of the devotional formulas – is to be found in the writings of the Venerable Hsüan Hua, Abbot of Gold Mountain Monastery, San Francisco. It does not solve the riddle just discussed, for the Master was not elucidating that point, but it does reveal that the purpose of reciting the sacred name is very different from that underlying most of the theistic practices with which it has been erroneously confused. Speaking of the recitation of Amitābha Buddha's name, he says: 'If you maintain your recitation morning and night without stopping, you may recite to the point that you do not know you are walking when you walk, you feel no thirst when you are thirsty, you experience no hunger when you are hungry, you do not know you are cold in freezing weather, and you do not feel warmth when you are warm. People and *dharmas* (entities) are empty and you and Amitābha become one. "Amitābha Buddha is me and I am Amitābha Buddha." The two cannot be separated. Recite single-mindedly and sincerely without erroneous thoughts. Pay no attention to worldly concerns. When you do not know the time and do not know the day, you may arrive at a miraculous state.' He also says: 'Day and night we recite the Buddha's name and with each sound we think of Amitābha. The phrase "Namo" means "homage". To whom are we paying homage? Ultimately we pay homage to ourselves! On the day when you entirely forget yourself, the Amitābha of your own nature will appear.' These quotations are of course applicable to the similar invocation offered to Kuan Yin, which must not be mistaken for a crude endeavour to win a divinity's favour by flattery, but recognised as a powerful technique for banishing ego-born obscurations and coming face to face with – Mind.

Another illuminating saying by the same Tripitaka Master runs: 'As I have told you many times, the Dharma-door of Buddha recitation is false, and so are (those of) dyana (Zen) meditation and the Teaching School, the Vinaya (Discipline) School and the Secret (Esoteric) School. You need only believe in it and false becomes true; if you do not believe, then the true becomes false. . . . Everything is created from mind alone.' On the face of it, this seems absurd. How can the false become true just by believing it? Yet to the mystic it makes excellent sense, for he recognises that *any picture* of what lies beyond the range of conceptual thought is bound to be too poor an approximation to have intrinsic worth; therefore all ways of picturing the path and goal are of value only as *convenient stand-ins* for use until direct intuitive perception is attained. Viewing the matter thus, one can more easily understand wherein lies the efficacy of the rites for invoking Kuan Yin.

Yet, even should one concede this point in relation to recitation of the sacred name or of the Dhāranī of Great Compassion, he may have difficulty in accepting what is written in the Lotus Sūtra and also in the sutra expounding that dhāranī concerning Kuan Yin's power to save beings from individual perils such as shipwreck, fire, storm, wild beasts, devils and even litigation. It must of course occur to one that, were these powers real in a literal sense, then a small body of devout believers, of whom there are many, could have stopped the Japanese invasion of China or the subsequent advance of the Red Army by causing weapons to fall to pieces in the soldiers' hands! So, short of rejecting the claims made in those sutras, one is tempted to seek some less literal interpretation.

Do those brave words mean perhaps that calling upon Kuan Yin with one-pointed mind makes one impervious to cold, heat, hunger, thirst, etc., and leads to such total freedom from the bonds of 'self', such perfect identification of the individual's mind with Mind, that litigation and death by shipwreck or in a tiger's maw are to be feared no more than dreams? This rationalisation is convenient, but it does not take account of there having been too many instances of people being literally saved from disaster in the nick of time by calling on Kuan Yin for one to be able to discount them all as fabrications. What then? Can it be that absolute faith conjures from within oneself such powerful reserves in the face of danger that seemingly miraculous escapes do in fact occur; or is something more mysterious, more 'magical' involved?

Personally I like to think that the inner purport of the passages about Kuan Yin's saving powers may be, in part, as follows. Sustained contemplation of the Bodhisattva as the embodiment of pure compassion inevitably affects the devotee's whole being. Seeking no advantages for himself, delighting to put himself out for others when urged to do so, he comes in some ways to resemble the Taoist sages of old – men so ungreedy, so easily satisfied with simple joys, so loath to take offence or put themselves forward unless pressed, so far removed from every kind of aggressive behaviour and factionalism that they were able to pass their lives in serene obscurity. Attracting no unwelcome attentions from robbers, government authorities or policemen, making no enemies, harbouring no grudges – in short, causing not the least offence to humans, animals or ghosts, they lived from day to day untroubled by savage beasts or extortioners, safe from the prisoner's manacles and strangers to the glittering horror of the executioner's sword. These were the 'Immortals whom ice could not freeze nor sunbeams scorch'. Calamities rarely if ever came their way. But whether this interpretation presents more than a fraction of the sutras' true meaning, I do not know.

In a commentary on the *Dhāranī Sūtra*, the Venerable Hsüan Hua relates a typical story of Kuan Yin's saving power. A certain devotee of hers was passing the night at an inn where the landlord was in the habit of administering drugged wine to the wayfarers who sought his hospitality and stealing into their rooms by night to rob and even murder them. This particular guest, however, was too faithful a Buddhist to touch wine; not being drugged, he awoke to find the landlord advancing upon him knife upraised; but at that very moment came a heavy banging at the front door. Hurriedly withdrawing, the landlord opened up to find a burly policeman-like individual who politely asked him to convey to one of his guests – the very one he had been on the point of murdering – that an old friend of such-and-such a name desired him to drop by in the morning. Tremblingly discarding his fell intention, he delivered this message soon after it was light. The wayfarer, though he gave no sign, had no difficulty in recognising the syllables of the visitor's 'name' as a quotation from the Dhāranī of Great Compassion. In other words, the policeman-like individual had either been Kuan Yin herself or a being sent by her to protect a good man who had long made a practice of reciting that dhāranī!

That the Venerable Hsüan Hua should in one place equate the celestial Buddhas and Bodhisattvas with the devotee's own mind and in another relate a factual story of Kuan Yin's saving power well illustrates the difficulty of arriving at a satisfactory conception of the nature of those celestial beings.

Chapter 6

Sacred Rites

The mysterious sound of Kuan Yin's name
Is holy like the ocean's thunder –
No other like it in the world!
Lotus Sūtra

During my early years in China, I once journeyed down the Cassia River, having taken passage on a wooden vessel much larger than a sampan but not so large as to be properly called a junk. On the first part of the trip the sails were mostly furled, little canvas being needed to carry it through those swift waters, still less the great sweeps lying along the gunwales to either side. The powerful current had been a curse and was now a blessing to the crew (a grandfather, his two sons, their wives and several children) for, old and young, they had performed the up-river journey trudging doggedly along the slippery bank, bodies bent double as they hauled at the ropes harnessing them like draught-horses to their boat. Setting out from Kweilin by moonlight, we awoke to find ourselves amidst the weird beauty of Yang Su's grotesquely convoluted mountains, of which a Chinese proverb says: 'Though Kweilin's scenery is unequalled in this world, Yang Su's is even better', which may be taken to imply that Yang Su is part of heaven. If so, then heaven is a place very well worth visiting.

Among my fellow-passengers was a black-gowned, shaven-headed, wizened little person who looked so wise that one might easily suppose him a great Tripitaka Master rather than an ordinary monk. Inspired by this man's charm and the magic of those extraordinary surroundings, I spoke to him freely of the affinity that had drawn me to Kuan Yin, my doubts about the claims

made in some of the texts recited in her honour and my being
baffled by the varying accounts of her true nature. Having listened attentively, he replied:

'You think too much.' Then, holding up a lotus flower he
had picked at dawn for his devotions, he exclaimed: 'Kuan Yin
is here in front of your nose. Smell!'

Though he said no more on the subject, I recognised that
one sentence as the most impressive sermon I had ever heard!
That the freshness arising in the early morning from dew lying
heavily upon the giant leaves carpeting a lotus pond is Kuan
Yin's fragrance, or that the lotus – spotless purity arising from
foetid mud – is pre-eminently her symbol, had not, I am sure,
as much as entered his head. Quite simply he had told me that,
in order to know her, I should yield my whole being to direct
experience, to the sacred rites, for example, to the chanting of
those passages I doubted, to the sonorous clang of bronze, the
staccato throb of the wooden-fish drum, the golden candle-light
playing upon her image and *whatever else might manifest itself*
to a mind properly receptive; if allowed to work their magic
unimpeded, these would best reveal the Bodhisattva's real
nature.

His advice recurred to me through the years as opportunities
for following it arose. Now and then, when left to my own
devices in some house where I was a guest, I would be struck
by a sudden intimation of Kuan Yin's presence and know without looking that, behind a screen or in some recess or corner
partly concealed from the rest of the room, stood a shrine to
her. Perhaps it would prove to be a trifling affair – just a foot-
wide altar-shelf or a glass and blackwood cabinet no larger than
a fair-sized tea caddy containing a small statue of her in snowy
porcelain, a miniature incense-burner, a pair of tiny candle-
sticks and a couple of little flower-vases to match, flowers and
a few pretty trifles reminiscent of the sea such as ornaments
of pearl or coral. Even if smoke were still arising from an incense
stick lit for morning or evening devotions, I would know that
that was not the reason for my apprehension of her presence,
since house-shrines may contain a likeness of any one of China's
innumerable deities and yet arouse no sense of a brooding
presence.

At times the experience would be so powerful that, had she

suddenly materialised, I would have deemed that almost less miraculous than the fact of her actually being there and yet not palpable to my senses. This occurred more than once during my visits to places known as 'halls of virtue' – a great feature of South China. Serving occasionally as homes for the aged, but more often as dwellings for communities of men or women living in semi-retirement from the world, they were to be found in the suburbs of many cities, as they are to this day in those parts of Southeast Asia with large Chinese communities. One comes upon an ornamental gateway giving access to some pleasant spot where upward-sweeping roofs peep from among a grove of trees. They are in fact small temples backed by court-yards with dormitories or rows of cell-like rooms occupied by recluses who may be dressed in sober monastic gowns. One's sense of Kuan Yin's actual presence has nothing to do with the appearance of her shrine or the architectural features of the sur-roundings, because very similar places may give one the feeling that she is not and has never been there; she is drawn, I think, by the purity of the inmates, their unassuming simplicity, their endeavours to live compassionately thinking no harm to the smallest insect let alone eating animal flesh, and the gentleness of their ways to one another and all about them. One has but to look into their eyes to know the fruits of devotion to Kuan Yin.

This attitude of joyous devotion is also prevalent in Japan, where Kuan Yin Bodhisattva goes by the name of Kwannon-sama. My favourite memories of a recent visit to that country are of bands of pilgrims plodding on foot from one holy place to another in a pleasantly wooded, mountainous region. Their white pilgrim surcoats gleamed like patches of snow against the sombre green of giant pines and cedars towering above a grey expanse of massive curving roofs. In those solitary places, except for the cries of birds or the soothing sound of water tum-bling down a slope, a marvellous stillness reigns – a stillness made all the more impressive by contrast with the occasional boom of an age-green temple bell of vast proportions. But with the pilgrims comes a sudden spate of cheerful noise – shuffling foot-falls, the thud of pilgrim staves upon the rugged path, the tinkle of the bells they carry suspended from their garments and the laughing chatter of simple folk who feel perfectly assured that every step of the way brings them nearer to rebirth in Amida (Amitābha)'s or Kwannon-sama's Pure Land. The joyful serenity of their faith is often expressed in tiny fragments of song known as *waka*, which are longer than *haiku* but just as rich in delicate allusions. These include some songs in honour of Kwannon-sama, of which the appropriate one is sung on arrival at each of thirty-three temples containing notable images of that Bodhisattva. For example:

'The spirit wishing for the next life may be light.
Not so the Buddha's pledge, firm as a rocky mountain.'

or

'Having left our native place and come at last to this Kimiye-dera temple, how close are we now to the Capital!' [*wherein the last word, though seemingly signifying Kyoto, means in fact the Pure Land to which Kwannon-sama will surely lead them*]

Another of these little songs implies that Kwannon-sama, by graciously transforming ordinary appearances, provides pilgrims with a foretaste of the beauty of her Pure Land. It runs:

'Looking again this morning, I realised it was but morning dew upon the moss in this Oka-dera temple garden – it was just like shining crystal!'

Yet another, addressed to Jundei – one of the many-armed forms of Kwannon-sama – stresses absolute conviction of the reliability of her vow to deliver all beings, no matter what their failings:

'However great our load of evil karma, it surely can be remedied by prayer – so firm this Jundei Hall!'

I am sure Japan contains many erudite Buddhists who share the more subtle Chinese interpretations of Kuan Yin's nature, but I know too little of them to be able to adduce as many comparisons with the Bodhisattva's devotees in China as I could wish.

To witness a full-scale performance of Kuan Yin's rites, it is best to visit a large temple, whether in China or Japan or one of the neighbouring countries, during any of three great annual festivals which fall respectively on the nineteenth day of the second, sixth and ninth lunar months. First comes her 'birthday' (a surprising term when one reflects that she is not a historical personage but born of a ray of light issuing from Amitābha Buddha's eye); next comes the feast celebrating her vow to renounce Nirvāna's final peace while any beings still wander in samsara's round; and then follows the feast celebrating her assumption of Bodhisattvahood. Once I was fortunate enough to witness such a festival at a large temple on the sea-coast in the vicinity of Amoy, a place with the usual lovely Chinese roofs but notable for walls built of red brick instead of grey. Cleanliness being considered an essential counterpart of inner purity, the Hall of the Three Buddhas and the special shrine to Kuan Yin had received such a sweeping and a scouring that not a speck of dust was to be found there. Moreover, the nuns and lay-recluses who had come in from round about to join the monks in celebrating the festival had made a point of taking a ritual bath – but whether or not in the sea, I do not remember.

When the time came for the great evening rite, candles blazed, clouds of perfumed smoke rose from a dozen censers disposed throughout the public parts of the temple, and the altars were decked with a rich profusion of fruit and flowers. Those taking part belonged to four separate communities – monks with jade-clasped *kasa* (togas) of brown silk or fine cloth worn over full-sleeved gowns of black cotton in a fashion that recalled the yellow robes worn by Buddhist monks in tropical countries; nuns, also shaven-headed and in black robes but with discernible hints of gleaming white under-jackets at throat and sleeves, an unwonted smartness appropriate to the occasion; female recluses in ceremonial robes of plain white; and ordinary people like myself, dressed for the most part in traditional Chinese silken gowns, but not without a sprinkling of men in Western-style suits. All but this last group had certainly purified themselves not merely by ablutions, but also by a period of silent contemplation to banish worldly thoughts and every other kind of thought extraneous to the rites. The appearance of the whole assembly was clean and richly sombre, there being no ostentation of any kind.

Summoned by the thunder of a giant drum, the devotees
went to their appointed places, monks on the right of the
assembly with the ordinary laymen behind them, nuns on the
left backed by the white-gowned recluses. Each, on reaching
his kneeling cushion, fell thrice to his knees touching head to
the ground; and, when a signal rang out from the bronze sound-
ing-bowl, this triple obeisance was repeated in unison. Though
at least two hundred people took part and the obeisance is a
complicated one, their movements were beautifully syn-
chronised to accord with signals made by several kinds of metal
percussion instrument. So in days gone by had the mandarins
prostrated themselves before the Son of Heaven at the dawn
levee in the Forbidden City.

Now a sweet and lingering note was struck; to the throb of
an enormous wooden-fish drum the incense paeon arose, a
solemn succession of long-drawn cadences more varied than a
chant and yet not quite a song. Addressed not to Kuan Yin but
to the Dharma Lord (the Buddha), it placed the rites in their
proper perspective; for, to her Buddhist followers at least, Kuan
Yin is not the central deity of a separate cult and her worship
conforms in all respects with the teaching and practice of
Mahayana Buddhism.

> Excellent fragrance,
> Glowing in the precious tripod,
> Permeates the universe,
> An offering to the Dharma Lord.
> May he blessedly endure
> For as long as sky and earth shall last!
> May he blessedly endure
> For as long as sky and earth shall last!
>
> Hail to the Bodhisattvas
> Borne upon these perfumed clouds!
>
> The effulgence of holiness and virtue
> May be likened to these spreading clouds.
> The Bodhi-Mind, immeasurably vast,
> Spreads forth its shining filaments.
> We pay reverence to the Dharma Lord,
> Praying that all may be auspicious.

> Hail to the Bodhisattvas
> Within this canopy of perfumed clouds!

At various stages of the rites came other chants conducive to the state of mind which they were intended to promote. Possibly they included a curious little paeon consisting of ten brief ejaculations used with mantric force to make an impact at the level beyond discursive thought, each consisting (in the original Chinese) of from two to four terse syllables:

> Kuan Shih Yin!
> Hail, Buddha!
> In him, a cause!
> In him, an outcome!
> Buddha-Dharma-Sangha outcome!
> Lasting joy, ego cleansed!
> Morning, think Kuan Yin!
> Evening, think Kuan Yin!
> Each call from mind!
> No call not mind-born!

Clearly one *could* draw some kind of connected meaning from these ejaculations, but it would be ludicrously inept and convey no idea of the effect at which the words are aimed.

Presently silence fell and the assembly made ready to recite the P'u Mên Chapter of the Lotus Sūtra, which everyone surely knew by heart as it is customary for devotees to recite it every day of their lives. First comes a section in prose which relates how the Bodhisattva Aksayamati made a formal enquiry about Kuan Yin's saving powers, to which the Buddha replied at length. Next Aksayamati recites some stanzas which summarise both his question and the Blessed One's reply. As the prose and verse sections cover more or less the same ground, I shall give only the verse portion here, having translated it from Tripitaka Master Kumārajīva's Chinese rendering of the original Sanskrit, made in the third century AD. In monosyllabic Chinese, the lines contain only five syllables each; recited rhythmically and rapidly with great fervour, they produce a much more powerful effect than can be hoped for from the English version. The eerie sounds beating upon the ear, the brilliant lights upon the altar fading into flickering shadows beneath a lofty roof and the heavy odour of flowers and incense combine to create a magical atmosphere in which the miracles recited appear more credible. Towards the end, the rhythm quickens and, when the passage commencing 'True Kuan Yin! Pure Kuan Yin!' is reached, it changes from five equal beats to a rapid $--//\cup\cup-$ which has a thrilling sound when pounded upon a great block of carved and lacquered wood that gives forth a deep, hollow resonance. As the short lines with a strongly marked caesura still follow in rapid succession, there is a feeling of mounting ecstasy:

> World-Honoured Lord and Perfect One,
> I pray thee now declare
> Wherefore this holy Bodhisat
> Is known as Kuan Shih Yin?
> To this the Perfect One replied
> By uttering this song:
>
> The echoes of her holy deeds
> Resound throughout the world.
> So vast and deep the vows she made
> When, after countless aeons
> Of serving hosts of Perfect Ones,
> She voiced her pure desire
> (To liberate afflicted beings).
>
> Now hearken to what came of it —
> To hear her name or see her form,
> Or fervently recite her name
> Delivers beings from every woe.
>
> Were you with murderous intent
> Thrust within a fiery furnace,
> One thought of Kuan Yin's saving power
> Would turn those flames to water!
>
> Were you adrift upon the sea
> With dragon-fish and fiends around you,
> One thought of Kuan Yin's saving power
> Would spare you from the hungry waves.

Suppose from Mount Suméru's peak
Some enemy should cast you down,
One thought of Kuan Yin's saving power
And sun-like you would stand in space.

Were you pursued by evil men
And crushed against the Iron Mountain,
One thought of Kuan Yin's saving power
And not a hair would come to harm.

Were you amidst a band of thieves,
Their cruel knives now raised to slay,
One thought of Kuan Yin's saving power
And pity must restrain their blows.

Suppose the King now wroth with you,
The headsman's sword upraised to strike,
One thought of Kuan Yin's saving power
Would dash the sword to pieces.

Were you close pent by prison walls,
Your wrists and ankles bound with chains,
One thought of Kuan Yin's saving power
Would instantly procure release.

Had you imbibed some fatal draught
And lay now at the point of death,
One thought of Kuan Yin's saving power
Would nullify its poison.

Were you beset by raksa-fiends
Or noxious dragons, gibbering demons,
One thought of Kuan Yin's saving power
And none would dare offend you.

Did savage beasts press all around
With fearful fangs, ferocious claws,
One thought of Kuan Yin's saving power
Would send them helter-skelter.

Should serpents lie athwart your path
Exhaling noxious smoke and flame,
One thought of Kuan Yin's saving power
Would make them vanish fast as sound.

Should thunder roll and lightning flash,
Or fearsome rains come hissing down,
One thought of Kuan Yin's saving power
Would straightway lull the storm.

Though beings oppressed by karmic woes
Endure innumerable sorrows,
Kuan Yin's miraculous perception
Enables her to purge them all.

Imbued with supernatural power
And wise in using skilful means,
In every corner of the world
She manifests her countless forms.

No matter what black evils gather –
What hell-spawned demons, savage beasts,
What ills of birth, age, sickness, death,
Kuan Yin will one by one destroy them.

True Kuan Yin! Pure Kuan Yin!
Immeasurably wise Kuan Yin!
Merciful and filled with pity,
Ever longed-for and revered!

O Radiance spotless and effulgent!
O night-dispelling Sun of Wisdom!
O Vanquisher of storm and flame!
Your glory fills the world!

Your pity is a shield from lightning,
Your compassion forms a wondrous cloud
Which, raining down the Dharma-nectar,
Extinguishes the flames of woe.

To those enmeshed in litigation
Or trembling in the midst of hosts
There comes the thought of Kuan Yin's power,
Whereat all hatred is dispersed.

The mysterious sound of Kuan Yin's name
Is holy like the ocean's thunder –
No other like it in the world!
And therefore should we speak it often.

Call upon it, never doubting,
Kuan Shih Yin – sound pure and holy;
To those who stand in mortal fear
A never-wavering support.

To the perfection of her merits,
To the compassion in her glance,
To the infinitude of her blessings,
Worshipping, we bow our heads!

Even more impressive was the recitation of the Dhāranī of Great Compassion that followed upon the chanting of the sutra. Known in Chinese as the Ta Pei Chou, it is a mantric utterance and held to be the most powerful means of invoking Kuan Yin. Like all mantras, it yields very little connected verbal sense even in the original Sanskrit and none at all in the Chinese transliteration of the syllables – or, at least, none perceptible to the vast majority of those who recite it. The Venerable Hsüan Hua has in fact extracted a meaning from every character, but perhaps to be taken as a list of psychic or yogic correspondences rather than as a translation. The apparent meaninglessness of the sounds is held to enhance rather than detract from a mantra's power, since reciting mantras lead the mind to an exalted level beyond conceptual thought at which, were one to be occupied with meaning, the sonorous syllables instead of promoting objectless awareness would stand in the way of its attainment. The Sanskrit text that follows here is Dr Suzuki's reconstruction of the lost original from the Chinese transliteration:

Namo ratna-trayāya namaḥ ārya avalokiteśvarāya bodhisatt-
vāya mahasattvāya mahākaruṇikāya oṃ sabalavati śudhanatasya
namas-kṛivanimaṃ ārya avalokiteśvara lamtabha namo nīlakaṇṭha śrīmahapataśami sarvatodhuśuphem asiyuṃ sarvasada nama
bhaga mabhatetu tadyathā oṃ āvaloki lokate kalati eśili mahā-
bodhisattva sabho sabho mara mara maśi maśi ridhayuṃ guru
guru gamam turu turu bhaśiyati mahā bhaśiyati dhara dhara
dhiriṇi śvaraya jala jala mama bhamara mudhili edhyehi śina
śina alaśim bhalaśari bhaśa bhaśiṃ bharaśaya hulu hulu pra
hulu hulu śrī sara sara siri siri suru suru budhi budhi budhaya
budhaya maitriye nīlakaṇṭha trisarana bhayamaṇa svāhā sitaya
svāhā mahā sitaya svāhā sitayaye śvaraya svāhā nīlakaṇṭhi svāhā
pranila svāhā śrī sidha mukhaya svāhā sarva mahā astaya svāhā
cakra astaya svāhā padma keśaya svāhā nīlakaṇṭhe paṇṭalaya
svāhā mobholiśaṅkaraye svāhā namo ratna-trayāya namaḥ ārya
avalokita īśvaraya svāhā oṃ sidhyantu mantra pataye svāhā

So powerful is this dhāranī, especially when recited under
such circumstances as those I am describing, that one's consciousness, borne aloft by the flow of mantric sound, soars
upwards to a sphere of marvellous luminosity. Its effect that
evening made it easy to believe the passage in the sutras assert-
ing that, when the Bodhisattva Kuan Yin first pronouned it
before the Buddha and his entourage of Bodhisattvas, devas,
humans, celestial creatures and spirits, the whole earth
trembled.

The high point of Kuan Yin's festival, however, was the invocation of her name, a practice never omitted from rituals of
that kind. Standing in serried ranks before the altar, the
assembly began to chant *Namo Kuan Shih Yin P'u-Sa* (Hail
to Kuan Shih Yin Bodhisattva) in unison over and over again,
starting at a slow and solemn tempo that gradually quickened.
In response to a note struck upon some sweet-voiced chiming
instrument, monks, nuns, white-clad recluses and ordinary
laymen in that order slipped from their places to form a single
file for circumambulation. Like a great serpent coiling and
recoiling upon itself, the long file wound its way about the
temple hall, sometimes circling the altar, sometimes the
statues behind it, always turning clockwise. Presently the
rhythm grew so rapid that the patter of cloth-soled feet all but

changed to a run, at which point the wording of the chant was shortened to a terse and urgent *Kuan Yin P'u-Sa, Kuan Yin P'u-Sa*.... From the faces of the devotees, I judged that many were experiencing a manifestation of the Bodhisattva in their minds. Then came another sweet chime, whereat the serpentine line diminished as, one by one, the members of each group slipped back to their former places. The chant, mounting to a crescendo, ceased abruptly amidst a silence loud enough to hear. Who could say in how many of those present ego-born delusion had given way to a glowing serenity, a state of keen but objectless awareness as though a brilliant ray were shining out upon a vast expanse of snow?

Strangely, no other practice within the entire range of methods for arousing *prajñā* (supreme wisdom) has received such a hostile reception in the West as this one, despite the warm acclaim of the Ch'an (Zen) Masters and Tibetan Lamas whom so many Westerners revere. Somehow its immense yogic value has escaped them. But why? Ideally one would suppose that children of the West, well trained in making a scientific approach to the study of new subjects, would be eager to experiment with *all* the yogic methods taught in the East, instead of rushing to conclusions and vociferously extolling some while rejecting others without trial.

It is true, however, that in the Far Eastern countries where the value of such yogic recitations is fully accepted, opinions as to how, why and under what conditions the practice is effective differ widely. For example, in China it is generally (though not universally) supposed that invocation of the sacred name, unless accompanied by at least a firm determination to cultivate compassion and, above all, to avoid causing pain or suffering to others, will not be effective; whereas in Japan there are numbers of devotees belonging to one or another of the Pure Land sects there who hold that the yoga owes its power solely to the vast merit of Amitābha Buddha or Kuan Yin, as the case may be, from which it follows that the moral state of the devotee is immaterial. That this view is sometimes held even in China is illustrated by the following curious story, which was told me not long ago by a Taiwan official during a visit to Bangkok.

'As a child I was deeply attached to my mother, who easily persuaded me to recite Kuan Yin's holy name hundreds of times over at dawn and sunset, as well as during idle moments at any time of day. I did it not only to please her, but because I took for granted that anything she recommended must be excellent. She was a wonderful person, both as wife and mother. Though she had adored my father during the twenty years or so of their marriage with a love that grew rather than diminished, she did not hesitate to select for him two unusually charming and talented concubines to give him the pleasure which, at her age, she could no longer provide herself. For months after the two girls arrived, she used to joke gaily about the way he doted on their youthful company, without a hint of jealousy. But when infatuation drove him to the point of allowing the elder of these girls to usurp the privileges of *T'ai-T'ai* (First Lady), she felt cruelly hurt. Uninterested in sexual love herself, she had supposed that my father's attachment to her would remain unchanged by his enchantment with mere beauty; besides, had she not herself provided the means of that enchantment as an act of love? Before long, the eighteen-year-old concubine had, with Father's connivance, made herself so important in the household that my mother was frequently humiliated before the servants – or even visitors! Sadly recognising that her husband no longer loved her and feeling she had nothing left to live for, she spent hours a day preparing for rebirth in a lotus that would one day open in Kuan Yin's paradise. To her joy, her strength soon failed and, within a year or so, she passed away.

'Naturally Father took care to give her the elaborate funeral befitting the *T'ai-T'ai* of a man in his position, but I believe the only grief he felt was on account of having to sleep apart from his concubines for a time as decreed by the ancient rules of decorum by which the obsequies of the dead are governed. As for me, my eyes were red with weeping; but, not daring to show anger against my father, I turned against Kuan Yin!

' "Kuan Yin Bodhisattva," I whispered fiercely, "you have taken away my mother with your empty blandishments! You *have* no Pure Land and there is no such thing as compassion in the world!" Does this seem an extreme reaction? Why had a woman so good and kind, a faithful devotee of the Compassionate One and as blameless as a human being can be, to suffer so? Why had modern education not opened my eyes to the obvious truth that everything connected with Kuan Yin was pure superstition? From the time of my mother's death, I abandoned repetition of the sacred name in sheer disgust.

'In those days I was living in Canton, working in the provincial Bureau of Foreign Affairs and making a name for myself by skilful handling of the British authorities in Hong Kong—men often arrogant towards us Chinese, but easy to get the better of because of their entire lack of subtlety. When they hectored us, we used to laugh behind our fans. On coming out of mourning I was married off to a pleasant girl of the Ch'ên family, chosen to cement a long-standing friendship between her father and mine. From being seriously put out by my father's refusal to permit me to select my own wife, I soon became fond of her – so fond that, as you will see, I was ready to do extreme violence to a person who presently tried to come between us. This person, as you may have guessed, was no other than my Second Mother, the upstart concubine who had besotted Father and driven Mother to her death. Pretending a genuine affection for my poor Ying, that lovely and abominable creature did everything in her power to undermine our love and respect for each other. What made it worse was that the woman had nothing to gain from such behaviour. She was motivated, I am sure, by a perverse fondness for mischief-making and for hurting anyone around her who happened to be vulnerable. You know the sort of woman I mean. Hong Kong seems to breed them. Did I tell you Mother had first come across her in Hong Kong? Brooding over the wretched business night and day, I became obsessed with the notion of ridding our family of the pretty monster – ridding the world of her, in fact! All I lacked was an absolutely safe means that would have no unfortunate effects on myself or Ying.

'The following year when the Pure Bright Festival came round, our whole family drove out of Canton to "sweep the tombs of our ancestors", which lay at an auspicious spot in the neighbouring hills, occupying a sizeable portion of one of the smaller cemeteries there. It was our custom to lay roast pork, boiled fowl and wine upon a stone table among the tombs as an offering to the august ancestral spirits, who sup upon the invisible essence of such meats. Later we would take home with us the coarse remains of the food from which the essence had been extracted and eat it ourselves. However, on that day Father decided we should have our memorial feast close by in a fold of the hills that offers a particularly fine view, but is isolated and out of sight of the crowds who flock to the cemetery for the festival. While we were sitting there eating and drinking, we noticed a dozen or so rascally fellows in shiny black pyjama-suits who looked like professional ne'er-do-wells. Standing some distance away, they were observing us closely and muttering to one another as though in two minds as to whether it would be safe to rob such a big party as ours or not. Presently they began closing in upon us; so my father, smiling meaningly, suggested to two of my uncles that they have a little target practice. Wine-jars were set up at a convenient distance and the three old men, drawing revolvers from their robes, shot the whole row to pieces with a single volley. By the time the echoes had died away, not one of those black-clad rascals was to be seen! They bothered us no more.

'Shortly after that I decided to stroll about to make sure that they were not lurking out of sight somewhere. So it happened that, quite by chance, I came upon my Second Mother who had apparently wandered towards the lonely spot where I found her, looking for a tree or bush – there are very few of them in those hills – behind which to relieve herself in suitably modest fashion. There was no one else in sight and nothing to prevent me from carrying out a plan that leapt fully formed into my mind, that of battering those lovely features into a pulp, burying her valuables and leaving her body on the hillside in full view of anyone who happened to pass by. Under the circumstances, no one would doubt that she had been murdered and robbed by the rascals we had seen staring at us during our meal. A long-sought opportunity to do away with her had been thrust by the gods into my hands! Why do you look so shocked? It is the plain duty of a good son to avenge his father or mother.

'My only problem was how to get really close without causing her alarm. She must have known very well how I felt about her and, were she to cry out, some of the others might come running up before I had had time to dispose of her jewellery to make it seem that she had been killed by robbers. As for a weapon, there were plenty of stones well suited to such work. Walking forward with a smile, I said: "Second Mother, it's not safe for you to wander alone like this. Supposing those people we saw just now—"

'While speaking I drew very close and, with my eye, marked the stone that would do my work. I am certain my face betrayed no hint of my intention—don't forget I had been a successful diplomat for some years. Yet somehow she divined what was passing in my mind and in turn communicated that knowledge to me. Oh no, she didn't scream or draw back—nothing of that sort. On the contrary, she stood very still and, favouring me with a beautiful smile that momentarily took all the hardness from her face, said placidly: "Chiu-k'u-chiu-nan Pu-Sa lai!" (Save-from-Suffering-Save-from-Harm Bodhisattva—come!)

'From lips accustomed to malice this prayer to Kuan Yin seemed so incongruous that I laughed as I made to seize her—or, rather, I opened my mouth to laugh and no doubt it stayed open in sheer amazement, for an iron paralysis had seized me. Hands raised to imprison her in such a way that her mouth would be tightly pressed against my chest to prevent her crying out, I stood as though turned to stone, unable to twitch an eyelid, much less carry out my plan. I have never seen a woman look so happy or so self-assured. Smiling pleasantly, she thanked me for coming to her aid and turned her back on me. As she walked off to rejoin the others, her laughter sounded like the tinkling of jade ornaments. Within seconds I regained my power of movement, but all thought of killing her had been shocked out of me forever. Who was I to pit my strength against the Bodhisattva's?

'You see how it is? That woman was thoroughly immoral, a creature full of malice amounting to cruelty, the very opposite of the common run of Kuan Yin's devotees. Yet she had triumphed over death for no other cause than absolute conviction of the compassionate Bodhisattva's desire to save every kind of sentient being whatsoever. Had Second Mother been a devil or a vampire fox, it would have made no difference. Kuan Yin's compassion extends to the worst of evil-doers, though of course she never assists them in their pursuit of evil. Always she endeavours to turn evil to good. For example, I resumed recitation of her holy name that very day and thanked her on my knees for saving me from murder. What is more to the point, but much less to be expected, Second Mother made no further attempts to estrange Ying from me and has more than once shown Ying a kindness at some little cost to herself. It may be that the Bodhisattva has not only saved her life but drawn her away from the path of cruelty and malice. I shall never get to like that woman but, as far as my knowledge goes, she has committed no further abominations since her life was spared. Father's passion for her has cooled and I sometimes wonder whether it is because she is probably a much nicer woman than she used to be.'

A monk to whom, without mentioning names, I passed on this story showed no surprise. 'We have always known that Kuan Yin saves *all* kinds of being,' was his quietly spoken comment.

That an amoral attitude to recitation of the sacred name is not widely shared in China is exemplified by a striking comment made not long ago by the Venerable Tripitaka Master Hsüan Hua when expounding the Heart of Great Compassion Dhāraṇī Sūtra, which introduces the dhāraṇī of that name. The sutra opens with the names and titles of a great assembly of the Buddha's disciples both human and supernatural which took place on Potala Mountain. Desiring to 'pacify and delight' all beings, the Bodhisattva Kuan Yin emitted golden rays whose brightness dimmed the sun and moon and, with the Blessed One's permission, proceeded to extol the dhāraṇī's merits in combating innumerable evils, casting out fear and fulfilling all longings. She recounted how, many aeons ago, she herself, on receiving the dhāraṇī from the Thousand-Rayed-Tathāgata-Who-Dwells-In-Stillness (unobscured Mind?), had immediately leapt from the first to the eighth stage of a Bodhisattva's progress and thereupon expressed this holy wish, 'If in time to come I am to obtain power to benefit all beings, may I now be endowed with a thousand hands, a thousand eyes', a wish that had been instantly fulfilled. She then declared to the assembly that those who cleave to the dhāraṇī will henceforth take rebirth from a lotus (i.e. in a Pure Land), never from a womb, but that cleaving to it entails voicing ten aspirations, namely that in a very short time one will: become acquainted with all the Buddha's teachings; attain the eye of wisdom; ferry all beings safely across samsara; perfect all manner of skilful means; embark on the vessel of supreme wisdom; escape from samsaric existence; attain to perfect conduct, perfect concentration and the Way; ascend Nirvāna's mountain; be free from conditioned activity; and unite with the Dharma–Nature–Body. So saying, she made these vows before the Buddha:

'World Honoured, should any being recite and cleave to the sacred Dhāranī of Great Compassion and yet fall into one of the three evil states of existence, I vow not to enter upon Supreme Enlightenment.

'Should any being recite and cleave to the sacred Dhāranī of Great Compassion and yet not be reborn in any Buddhaland, I vow not to enter upon Supreme Enlightenment.

'Should any being recite and cleave to the sacred Dhāranī of Great Compassion and yet not achieve the eloquence (born of) limitless samādhi, I vow not to enter upon Supreme Enlightenment.

'Should any being recite and cleave to the sacred Dhāranī of Great Compassion and yet not obtain in this very life the fruits of all that he desires, then he cannot have been (properly reciting and cleaving to) the Dhāranī of the Heart of Great Compassion. He should put away wrong-doing and put away insincerity.'

Having thus vowed, she averred that, by cleaving to the dhāranī, one may avoid all forms of untimely death and attain rebirth under conditions highly conducive to wise and virtuous living and the attainment of Enlightenment. Then did she communicate to the assembly the words of the sacred dhāranī, whereat the earth underwent six convulsions, jewelled flowers rained down, the Buddhas rejoiced and evil beings shuddered.

The fruit of uttering the dhāranī, she continued, is a heart (or *mind* – there is no distinction in Chinese) characterised by: vast compassion, equanimity, freedom from unconditioned activity, absence of all defilements and attachments, ability to contemplate the Void, reverence, humility, no confusion, no disposition to cling to (dualistic) views, and a plenitude of unexcelled Bodhi. However, one must first vow to deliver all sentient beings, strictly observe the precepts and abstain from the flesh of sentient creatures, for only then will Kuan Yin bestow protection. The sutra then provides instructions for the mantric use of the dhāranī in combating specific evils, commanding spirits, curing maladies and so forth. It closes with the Buddha extolling the dhāranī to a rejoicing assembly.

The language is hauntingly picturesque, but the content, though it inculcates the loftiest ideals, may strike present-day readers as dwelling overly on magic, until they realise that, like the sacred tantras and other mystical texts, the wording is open to several levels of interpretation. The Venerable Hsüan Hua's striking comment ran more or less as follows: 'One who recites the dhāranī but is not compassionate is in effect *not* reciting the dhāranī; whereas one whose heart is filled with compassion *is* reciting it even though no words are uttered!'

One may object that this interpretation begs the question, for it seems quite apparent that people so compassionate as to be deemed to be reciting the dhāranī unceasingly in the Venerable Hsüan Hua's sense do not in fact obtain the advantages promised by the sutra. But do they not? In Southeast Asia, at a certain time of the year, many thousands of Buddhist monks betake themselves one by one to the solitude of jungle or mountain, but never has one heard of their being bitten by snakes or mauled by wild animals. Benevolent to all beings, they abide in the jungles untroubled by thoughts of peril. So, too, does a layman by nature too unworldly to be capable of factionalism or of espousing political, religious or other causes, live out his life without having reason to fear the vile attentions of CIA agents, or of the authorities who imprison dissidents in concentration camps or 'liquidate' them. In this sense, at least, the doors of prisons gape and the executioner's sword is shattered.

Chapter 7

Contemplative Yogic Meditation

Therefore should the mind be constantly fixed on her
Lotus Sūtra

Sheltered by a horseshoe-shaped hill in the heart of the Shan
tung orchard country is an ancient Buddhist temple I was
especially fond of visiting for long weekends. It is approached
by a stone-paved path that winds past mile upon mile of fruit
trees which, in spring, are clothed with many-coloured blossom
and, in autumn, are bowed by their loads of peaches, plums
and *sha-li* pears. One comes at last to the hill and recognises
its jagged ridge from a hundred Chinese paintings of such
scenery, for the Chinese eye delights in convoluted rocks and
sees in them a whole menagerie of improbable animals – here
a couple of *shih-tzu* lions sporting with each other, there a tiger
playing benevolently with a turtle, somewhere else a handsome
ch'i encountering its *lin*, these last being respectively the male
and female of that extraordinary and illustriously omened
creature, the Chinese 'unicorn'.

The temple, once patronised by emperors, has long fallen on
hard times and, in the mid-1930s, boasted but a single monk.
Aged about fifty, he wore a roughly patched gown and, being
of Shantung peasant stock, might have been taken for an unlettered countryman employed as temple caretaker, but for his
eyes, which told another story. So narrow that the irises were
half-concealed, they shone with humour and intelligence and
the lids had besides an elastic quality, for suddenly the eyes
would grow round and surprisingly large like a demon's. I think

putting on a daemonic face gave him enjoyment, besides adding force to whatever he happened to be impressing on someone. The first time we met, I had recently come from South China with my questions about Kuan Yin's true nature unresolved. One evening, after a meal of cooked vegetables, millet soup and coarse, reddish rice, I spoke of my affection for that Bodhisattva and of how taking part in her rites uplifted me, although I was never very sure why that should be so.

'Rites!' he exclaimed, smiling as though at some secret joke. 'Recitation of the Lotus Sūtra? The Dhāranī of Great Compassion? Invoking the sacred name? All very, very good, if you are lazy or too involved with the world of dust to undertake things seriously. You, since your affinity with the Bodhisattva must stem from former lives, should do better than that – unless you know their *true* significance and the manner of making them bear fruit – that, of course, is quite another thing. Meanwhile, if you desire to know the Bodhisattva, meditate! Without meditation, studying the Buddha's teaching is like learning sword-play without so much as a stick in your hand, like learning archery with a splendid bow but not an arrow in your quiver!'

'I *do* meditate!' I answered indignantly, being young enough then to resent any underrating of what I thought my rather creditable progress, especially if one made allowances for my being a foreign devil-man still fairly new to such things.

'Ah, *then*!' he breathed, pretending to be mightily impressed. 'May this humble monk venture to ask you, Sir, just how it is done. I am all eagerness to learn from you.'

'Your Reverence!' I remonstrated, stung by the harshness of his irony, but proceeded to relate with moderate satisfaction how I had tried and discarded one method of meditation and then learnt from an old nun a method that seemed to suit me very well.

He listened, still with an ironical expression, eyes fixed intently on my face as though able to read what lay behind it, their twinkling orbs glinting in the light of the table-lamp. His manner irked me and, in the silence that followed, I waited for his comments feeling ill at ease. His reply, when it came, was as terse and unsympathetic as it was abrupt. 'Seven parts good!' he shouted, eyes blazing and round as a long-tongued demon's. His meaning baffled me, 'seven parts in eight' being the Chinese idiom for 'nine out of ten'. I sat mulling it over when, all of a sudden, his forefinger shot out and was levelled at my face like a sword. 'Only the eighth part counts', he added severely and then unaccountably roared with laughter until, seeing he had hurt me, he said more gently: 'Good friend, good friend, no need to be startled by this boorish know-nothing, but you do see why seven parts is just the same as no parts.' Nodding towards the tea-kettle simmering on its charcoal stove, he added: 'The water there may be seven parts heated, for all I know, but until it is just on the boil, what sort of tea could you make with it? You meditate zealously, devotedly – I am sure of it – but has Kuan Yin confirmed your success?'

'Well – ah – that is – you mean I should expect a vision?'

'*P'ei!*' he snorted contemptuously. 'What use could you make of that! I meant do you know, now, who she is?'

'That', I answered sadly, 'is just what I long to know and –'

' – and hope I shall tell you,' he broke in playfully, 'as though human speech were deva language. Well, I'll tell you *how*. All you have to do is leap across samsara's bitter ocean in one bound, as Monkey once leapt from the Buddha's finger, and pay a visit to your original mind. So now you know *how*. As for *where*, that is more difficult, for mind's abiding place is nowhere, nor does it abide. Let the rolling ocean of thought be stilled. When your mind shines sun-like upon vast emptiness, the Bodhisattva will appear. *You* are the one to accomplish the eighth part, but don't forget to be grateful to your daddy here for reminding you to throw away the other seven. How was your walk this morning? Did you climb above the mist?'

This abrupt change of subject meant there was no more to be gained from him. Still, he had done a lot. It was just as well to be rid of absurd complacency about my 'progress' in meditation. Until the water in my kettle boiled, it might just as well remain stone cold. And yet? To boil, it must first get hot gradually. Or not? Who could fathom his meaning? Buddhists of the Ch'an (Zen) Sect had been talking about that problem for more than a thousand years without coming to any agreement.

What is specially interesting about our exchange that night is that here was a monk obviously trained in Ch'an who, instead of scornfully dismissing a Pure Land approach, saw the two as one. His remark about having to know the *true* significance of Pure Land rituals reveals that he believed them fully effective if properly understood and performed. Throughout China, I found this same regard for all sects and methods as valid means of coming face to face with truth. If this book has a particular message for Western Buddhists, it is: '*Do not fall into the trap of making distinctions that are meaningful only at a very superficial level. Ch'an, Pure Land and Vajrayana are not three paths to the same goal, but three gateways to the same path, or even one gateway seen in various lights.*'

In bed that night, pricked by the stubs of fresh grass with which pillow and mattress had been hurriedly stuffed on my arrival, but enjoying their fragrance, I reviewed the progress I had made so far. While in South China, I had begun by attempting one of the methods of meditation laid down in the Amitayus Sūtra, only to abandon it as beyond my capacity (or because, chance having never led me to sit at the feet of a Master of the Pure Land Sect, I had not known how to set about it rightly).

In that sutra, Kuan Yin appears as one of the Three Holy Ones who form the object of the eighth contemplation set forth there. One has to visualise three giant lotuses whereon stand an image of Amitayus (a form of Amitābha Buddha) flanked by those of Kuan Yin and Ta Shih Chih (Mahāsthāmaprāpta) Bodhisattvas; the rays of golden light emitted by their bodies illuminate innumerable jewelled trees; and, at the foot of these trees, appear identical images of those three beings countless in number. This feat of visualisation is nothing to what follows in the subsequent contemplations. In the tenth, for which the attention is directed wholly to Kuan Yin, her golden body has to be visualised as reaching a height of eight hundred million million yojanas or, according to some interpretations, eighty thousand million million! (Mr Charles Luk informs us that one yojana is the equivalent of a day's march for an army, but even if it were only a few centimetres, the total height would be quite beyond human conception.) Within the Bodhisattva's halo are to be seen five hundred Buddhas in Nirmānakāya form, *each* with a following of five hundred others in Sambhogakāya form and an incalculable number of devas. Between the Bodhisattva's eyebrows is a curl of seven colours emitting rays of eighty-four thousand hues, in every one of which are countless Nirmāna-kāya Buddhas each surrounded by innumerable Sambhogakāya

Buddhas! Each of the Bodhisattva's finger-tips has eighty-four thousand very distinct lines – and so on! The sheer magnitude was dismaying. Of course many people do perform such visualisations and it may be that, had I been properly instructed at the time, I should not have been frightened away from them. I now know that the figures are not meant to be taken literally, the purpose being exactly that of Ch'an (Zen) koans, namely to stretch the mind beyond breaking point so that 'ordinary' consciousness gives way to extraordinary consciousness. However, this knowledge came to me too late with the result that I have never made a proper study of that technique or learnt from a competent Tripitaka Master what the adept is really expected to do. At the time I had decided without hesitation that the technique was not for me and had enquired diligently about more simple ones.

One day, during a visit to Canton, I had had an opportunity to question an old nun who had taken up temporary lodging in a dark cell within the precincts of Ta Fu Szû Monastery which for some reason was no longer functioning. My speaking to her, possibly with a touch of levity, about the hopelessness of trying to cope with those vast numbers had earned me a severe glance; but, being a kind old lady, she had handed me a cup of tea and said evenly: 'I don't know about that, Sir. The sutra puts it that way, so you may be sure there is a lot of sense to it. I do things otherwise because, being old and unlettered, I just have to do the best I can. You won't want to bother your head about the methods used by a useless old nun like me.'

'Wrong, Auntie. I am longing to know what you do. My friends told me you are devoted to Kuan Yin and so I have come specially to learn from you.'

The rheumy eyes had peered at me to see if I were mocking her, for she was as humble as she was old, a woman of peasant stock not used to being sought out by educated people, to say nothing of foreign devils like myself.

Satisfied, she had remarked: 'As you wish, Sir, though I can't think why your friends should have sent you to me. I expect you will be disappointed. Here, take this fan. The tea's made you sweat. Fanning will help to keep off the mosquitoes, too. Have you ever seen so many? Canton is full of greedy people.

That's why we have such swarms of mosquitoes, I sometimes think. Greedy people reborn, you know. It's a punishment all right. Mosquitoes seldom get enough to eat and, when they do find a good meal, the victim may squash them flat long before they've drunk their fill. What was I going to say? Oh yes, meditation – that was it.'

Talkative like many old people, she had embarked upon a rambling story about her youth, mentioning the name and appearance of her native village, the number and characteristics of her brothers and sisters, and a great many other things while I had fought a losing battle with those winged incarnations of greedy spirits; but gradually my interest had quickened. As a young girl she had been betrothed; the boy had been killed in a local squabble and she had come to Canton to earn her living as a servant. Nothing notable had happened to her until she was well into her fifties when her current mistress, blaming her for the loss of a jade bracelet, had given her a beating and driven her from the house. After that Ah Cheng, as she was called, had wandered about looking for work somewhere too far from Canton for the unjust charge of stealing to catch up with her. One night she had taken shelter in a temple dedicated to Kuan Yin where two nuns resided. In the middle of the night she had crept into the shrine-hall and addressed to the Bodhisattva a prayer in which despair was mixed with peasant cunning.

'Holy Kuan Yin, I'm done. No money for the boat tomorrow, no strength to walk to the next town, no money to stay here. Nothing. People say you help. I am not sure I believe them, so just show me it's true!'

While she was earning her breakfast by sweeping out the courtyard and doing various odd jobs the following morning, an irate-looking merchant came running in, shouting to no one in particular: 'Those rascals have left without me! Their mothers' – ! Now who's going to look after this little minx? Gets in the way all day long. I'd leave her here if one of you would take the price of her keep and a bit over to look after her till I come back. Any of you old black gowns willing, eh?'

There had been a mix-up. This coarse-mouthed but not ill-natured man had been stranded with some bales of cloth and a two-year-old niece a hundred *li* up river from his destination. Ah Cheng volunteered to go with him to look after the child and satisfied him so well that she remained in his service as nurse-housemaid until his death a few years later. During all that time she was treated as a human being and adequately paid! Never did she doubt that all this was due to Kuan Yin's intervention or fail to do reverence to the Bodhisattva morning and evening.

'At first, you understand, Sir, I just recited Her name. It wasn't enough. I wanted to *see* Her. So I asked at the temple in K'ai Ping how it could be done. A monk there taught me a fine method. You sit down on a hill-top or anywhere high enough for you to see nothing but the sky in front of your eyes. Otherwise a blank wall will do. With your mind you make everything empty. There's nothing there, you say. And you see it like that – nothing, emptiness. Then you say, ah but there *is* something. Look, there's the sea and the moon has risen – full, round, white. And you see it like that – sea, silver in the moonlight with little white-topped waves. In the blue-black sky above hangs a great moon – bright, but not dazzling – a soft brightness, you might say. You stare at the moon a long, long time, feeling calm, happy. Then the moon gets smaller, but brighter and brighter till you see it as a pearl or a seed so bright you can only just bear to look at it. The pearl starts to grow and, before you know what's happened, it is Kuan Yin Herself standing up against the sky, all dressed in gleaming white and with Her feet resting on a lotus that floats on the waves. You see Her, once you know how to do it, as clearly as I see you sitting there with the window behind you – clearer, because Her face is not in shadow, also Her robes are shining and there's a halo round Her head, besides the bigger oval-shaped halo cast by Her body. She smiles at you – such a lovely smile. She's so glad to see you that tears of happiness sparkle in Her eyes. If you keep your mind calm by just whispering Her name and not trying too hard, She will stay a long, long time. When She does go, it's by getting smaller. She doesn't go back to being a pearl, but just gets so small that at last you can't see Her. Then you notice that the sky and sea have vanished, too. Just space is left – lovely, lovely space going on for ever. That space stays long if you can do without you. Not you *and* space, you see, just space, no you.'

Towards the end of this, her eyes had closed; no doubt she

was actually seeing what she described. It was one of the deeply moving experiences of my life. Seeing her lie back against the chair, eyes still closed, I had decided I must at all costs avoid breaking in on her peace; so, leaving a little 'incense money' on the table, I had slipped quietly away.

I suppose one could write the instructions for performing that simplest and most beautiful of the Kuan Yin contemplations in the form used in manuals of meditation, but that would certainly be no improvement on the old nun's vivid description. It is a form of contemplation of which I have grown fond, though I doubt if I ever perform it as successfully as she did. After some forty years of giving thought to it, I cannot think of a single word that would add to the excellence of her way of putting it.

There are numerous contemplations similar to that one. For example, in Japan some Shingon adepts visualise a moon risen from the ocean very much as the old nun described it, in which suddenly appears the Sanskrit syllable HRI – Kuan Yin's bīja-mantra. From this HRI suddenly emerges the Bodhisattva and the rest of the meditation proceeds on rather similar lines to the one described. Clearly the most vital part – as with Tibetan Tara meditations – is the attainment of a state of void in which adept and void are one and indistinguishable; for thus the adept transcends the plane of relative truth and attains perception of truth's ultimate aspect – the Great Void. Each time this is done successfully, a further blow is struck at the persistent delusion of possessing a self. The longer and more frequently he abides in a state of no-self, the firmer becomes his perception of self's intrinsic voidness. In time, recognition of the delusory nature of the self is carried over into ordinary states of consciousness; so that, even when attending to the business of daily life, he retains that recognition in the depths of his mind. This, of course, has a powerful influence on his conduct; whoever works at his job in the full knowledge of selflessness is likely to perform his tasks perfectly, with the work being done for its own sake and no thought spared for any personal advantages to be reaped. Moreover, to act selflessly is to act compassionately, and compassion is precisely what is embodied in the concept of Kuan Yin. It follows that Kuan Yin, for all her superficial resemblance to the goddesses of other religions and to the Virgin

Mary, is not really to be thought of as a mother or a sovereign queen, but as a personification of the beneficent force that flows from Mind. Once this is grasped, the real point of Pure Land Buddhism is understood and whatever distaste one has hitherto felt for it is bound to wane. The supposition that, to use the words of a Western writer, it is 'the very antithesis of Buddhism as ordinarily understood' falls away.

In the words of an iconoclastic Tripitaka Master who I came upon years later in the midst of a sermon during a visit to Soochow: 'The (celestial) Bodhisattvas? Where and what are they? Do not look to find them among the beings in the six states of existence (gods, asuras, humans, animals, pretas and those passing through hell), nor among the three realms (of desire, form and formlessness), nor yet among the eighteen Brahmalokas (heavens), nor anywhere but in your own minds. To discover them, let your minds be still. In the stillness resides no particle of self or other. There, perceiving Manjusri (embodiment of wisdom), you will know him for Samantabhadra (action); perceiving Samantabhadra, you will know him for Kuan Yin!'

With the Cantonese nun's method of meditation, I made progress that seemed to me sufficient until my complacency was shattered by the orchard country monk. Many years later when I journeyed to the Indo-Tibetan border regions, I at last came upon a method of yogic contemplation in which I could exult since it promised startling progress, being a Short Path method for attaining Enlightenment in this very life. It was as well, though, that I had given up hoping for a clear exposition of Kuan Yin's true nature. That the Tibetan lamas knew little or nothing of the Bodhisattva by that name and in that form was of no significance, for I recognised her as being essentially an aspect of Avalokita and Tara, of whom they had much to teach; the trouble was that, like the Chinese monks I had questioned so persistently, they spoke of celestial Bodhisattvas now as beings existing independently, now as creations of our own minds. I believe the difference, so notable to one with Western upbringing, never even occurred to those holy men whose meditations had taught them a very different mode of thought, leading them to comprehend subtle truths beyond the understanding of ordinary, untrained minds.

At my special request, I received Tara – who is also Kuan Yin – as my *idam*. Henceforth, I learnt to centre my meditation on her, to see her not only as a projection of my own mind, but also as the being I might become through yogic union with her. With this sort of meditation one does not waste time enquiring into the real nature of the being invoked, who may at the outset be viewed in any way one chooses – as a goddess, for example. The essence of the practice is not to know that being, but to *become* her; with the merging of identities, all questioning will of course be set at rest, so there is no need for it in the first place.

How and why this particular method of yogic contemplation is so powerfully effective is difficult to describe; it must be accompanied by great changes in one's whole attitude of mind and inner life. On the other hand, the skilful means employed in the yoga could easily be set forth, were one authorised to teach it. What I feel able to say on the subject has already appeared in other books; but, by great good fortune, I have since come into possession of a Chinese yogic text pertaining to Kuan Yin herself, though I believe it to have once been a Tara contemplation and that, taken from a Tibetan source, it was subsequently adapted to Kuan Yin for use by her Chinese devotees. It is worth setting down, even if only as a literary curiosity, for such texts pertaining to *Kuan Yin* must be rare. Unfortunately it has been oversimplified, being indeed the simplest tantric *sadhana* I have ever seen, but this is no disadvantage to it as an illustration of the kind of yogic methods used in Vajrayana practice. Known as 'Three Kuan Yin Visualisations In One', it was rendered into Chinese from the Tibetan by the Venerable Abbot Jên Wên of the Monastery of Amrta (Sweet Dew) in Bangkok, and the following is my English translation of his text:

THREE KUAN YIN VISUALISATIONS IN ONE

PRELIMINARY

After cleansing body and mind, hold an incense-taper in the left hand and cause the finger and thumb of the right hand to form a circle by placing them tip to tip. Visualise at the point where thumb and finger meet a white OM. This suddenly

becomes a budding lotus with which one traces the syllables
OM AH HŪM over the tip of the incense-taper thus causing
the perfumed smoke to spread out forming an immeasurable
expanse of purity. Next, raising the incense-taper to the forehead with both hands, mentally repeat these words: 'May these
fragrant clouds form offerings to the Triple Gem, to the
Buddhas, Bodhisattvas and Gurus of the Ten Directions and
Three Times!' Having planted the taper in the censer with the
left hand, one now makes four prostrations, first to the Vajra
Guru, next to the Buddha, Dharma and Sangha in turn.

FIRST VISUALISATION
Sit before a statue of the Buddha, preferably in lotus posture,
otherwise in any comfortable position, so that the rite may be
performed tranquilly with a pure and peaceful mind. At the
crown of your head appears a white OM; in the region of your
throat, a red AH; close to your heart, a blue HŪM; these syllables emit rays of those three colours in all directions. Thereby
all the evil karma wrought by self and others since beginningless
time is expelled in the form of a black liquid which seeps into
the ground until not a drop is left. Thus are your body, speech
and mind transformed into the Body, Speech and Mind of
Kuan Yin, exquisitely lovely and overflowing with compassion.
Forming the lotus mudra (hands held at breast height, thumbs
and finger-tips together, but hands arching away from each
other as far as possible so as to resemble the two halves of a
lotus ≪ ≫), visualise the mantra OM MANI PADME HŪM
and cause the mind to revolve from syllable to syllable thus:

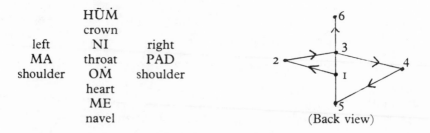

	HŪM	
	crown	
left	NI	right
MA	throat	PAD
shoulder	OM	shoulder
	heart	
	ME	
	navel	

(Back view)

Presently rearrange the syllables mentally and revolve the mind
from one to another thus:

	OṀ	
	crown	
left	MA	right
ME	throat	NI
shoulder	HŪṀ	shoulder
	heart	
	PAD	
	navel	

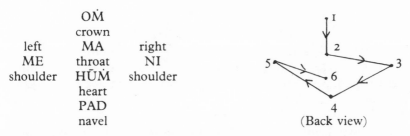

(Back view)

The more these revolving visualisations are repeated, the more marvellous the results.

SECOND VISUALISATION
Visualise within your breast a lunar disc, bright and pure within and without. Suspended in the void before you appears a pink lunar disc enshrining the syllable TAṀ, which is so immeasurably brilliant that it illuminates the entire realm of form. Suddenly this syllable is transformed into a likeness of Kuan Yin, white in colour, with one head and two arms; upon her head is a five-petalled lotus-crown on which can be seen likenesses of the five celestial Buddhas. Her legs are folded in the lotus posture. Pearls adorn her wrists and ankles. Three strands of jewelled ornaments encircle her neck. Upon her crown, a white OṀ; at her throat, a red AH; close to her heart, a blue HŪṀ, wherefrom rays of those three colours blaze down upon you. These, blending with the rays emitted by the OṀ AH HŪṀ adorning your own body, enter your head by an aperture at the apex of the crown which opens to receive them. The figure of Kuan Yin suspended in space before you now contracts; becoming very small, it follows the rays flowing in through the aperture at your crown and merges with your person so that you and she are one and indivisible.

Next, with the tips of the thumb and ring-finger of your right hand conjoined, trace the syllables OṀ AH HŪṀ on your left hand. Mentally create a pearl and, with your left hand, trace those same syllables upon its surface, simultaneously contemplating the syllables with your mind and uttering them with your lips. Then visualise yourself holding the pearl close to your breast with the thumbs and forefingers of both hands. Thus doing, softly recite the mantra OṀ MANI PADME HŪṀ (many times).

THIRD VISUALISATION

Visualise the syllable OM blazing upon your crown, pouring forth white rays and illuminating all sentient beings in the six states of existence so that their errors of body, speech and mind are purged. Shining in the region of your heart is a blue HŪM whose rays fill the whole earth, bringing comfort to all sentient beings. Within the circle of the light it sheds are to be seen as many Pure Lands as one cares to visualise. Then the white and the blue rays enter your crown and permeate to the lower region of your body. Using the same mudra as before, recite OM MANI PADME HŪM continuously. This done, rise and make three obeisances, chanting each time: 'Hail to the Bodhisattva Kuan Shih Yin!' Finally make three more obeisances, chanting: 'Hail to the Triple Gem, to the Eternal Buddhas, Dharma and Sanghas of the Ten Quarters!'

COLOPHON

The merit of performing this rite brings about the transformation of sentient beings everywhere. It obliterates the sufferings of the Three (lower) States of Existence and ensures swift achievement of Unexcelled Enlightenment.

(End of the rite)

The instructions given above are by no means as arbitrary as they may seem. The white OM, red AH and blue HŪM at crown, throat and heart respectively are encountered extensively in such yogas, for these sounds and colours are held to have vital correspondences with the psychic centres in those three parts of the body. Kuan Yin's or Avalokita's mantra OM MANI PADME HŪM is of course the best known of all mantras; and the directions for performing the *sadhana*, though much simpler than those for similar *sadhanas*, follow a similar pattern.

One cannot in a few paragraphs do justice to the subject of mantras. Suffice, then, to say that they are an essential support to the visualisations whereby adepts attain direct communion with the forces embodied in such concepts as Kuan Yin; and that the *sadhanas* containing them are among the most powerful yogic methods known. Though the written description of a *sadhana* may make it appear to be no more than a mental charade, it involves marvellous correspondences between the realms of form and Void.

Recitation of the sacred name, a practice I have described in connection with the rites, is properly speaking another form or equivalent of contemplative meditation and is the easiest way of attaining one-pointedness of mind. Some devotees manage to keep the sacred formula revolving in their minds day and night, so that it continues even when, at another level of consciousness, they are engaged in conversation or coping with the affairs of daily life. If one attempts this oneself, the first result is likely to be either that the repetition becomes mechanical or that one's attention to affairs becomes too perfunctory, but this difficulty can be overcome with practice, especially if one earns one's living in ways that do not require great concentration or much discursive thought. In time the sacred formula will continue to revolve in the mind even when one is asleep and dreaming. At moments of imminent danger, the mind remains calm; no threat to life or limb can cause a break in the chain of recitation.

A friend of mine was once bold enough to tell a well-known Tripitaka Master of the Pure Land Sect that, in his opinion, recitation of the sacred name is a practice too mechanical to be spiritually effective.

'Mechanical!' echoed the Master, immensely surprised. 'How can that be?' Gazing at my friend as though wondering whether he were perhaps dealing with a lunatic, he continued: 'Cleaving to the sacred name results smoothly and easily in one-pointedness of mind – the very state which is sought so arduously by meditators belonging to all the eight schools of Buddhism, to say nothing of Taoists, Hindus and others outside the Dharma. Attaining one-pointedness, you will, sooner or later according to your capacity, see your Buddha or Bodhisattva standing before you – a living being, garments fluttering, breast rising and falling with the breath of life; or, if that is not what you look for, you will enter the non-dual state and discover that, here in this world of form, you have attained to the great Void. Then will you know tangible forms for what they are – bubbles, mirages, dreams. Just as you are not now deceived by those snowy mountains hanging in the sky, knowing them as you surely do for clouds, so will you recognise each object as a *no-thing*, not unreal, but ever-changing, transient, devoid of own-being.'

'Good, Venerable, but what if I do behold the Bodhisattva standing before me, garments fluttering in the breeze? Beautiful and satisfying as that might be, would it not be just another illusory appearance?'

When the Tripitaka Master, overtaken by a gale of laughter, had recovered something of his gravity, he said pointedly: 'To certain people stuck like flies in the web of intellect, the experience should be especially edifying. Beholding your own thought-form smiling down at your bewilderment, surely you would reflect: "Since with my own mind I am able to create a beautiful lady, is there a single thing mind does not create, including this sky, this hill, this sea?" No longer will you doubt what is said in the sutras about the nature of this world. Hurrying to your library, if you have one, you will turn to those sutras and at last perceive their wisdom, eyes no longer dimmed by opaque clouds of intellectual vapour. From that day on, your studies will be fruitful!'

My friend was impressed; but, not averse to learning a little more from this forthright monk, he said: 'Does Your Reverence imply that people who have been spared an education see more clearly than others?'

'They will mostly see the Bodhisattva as a deity who has condescended to reward their pious recitations. Rejoicing, they will henceforth recite with redoubled fervour and assuredly be reborn in a Pure Land.'

The last sentence took my friend aback, making him wonder whether this monk was as wise as he had thought. For, as he told me afterwards, he had supposed that Pure Lands were dangled like carrots before people with insufficient intellectual capacity to imagine a less materialistic state. However, questions on this point produced such evasive answers that my friend was disappointed, supposing he had caught the monk out in some way. Personally, I believe that the monk, all too well aware of the harm done by definitions which demean and annihilate the more subtle kinds of concept, was simply following normal practice on such occasions, which is to discourage questions about what can be properly understood only when direct perception is attained. Herein, I am sure, lies the reason for the difficulty I had experienced in finding any learned monk who would express himself forthrightly on the subject of the Bodhisattvas' true nature and the real meaning of the term 'Pure Land'. Both are to be experienced, not talked about. Where words are bound to mislead, silence is best.

How fully invocation of the sacred name takes the place of the contemplative meditation practised by other sects can be seen from the fact that, just as Ch'an (Zen) monks from time to time attend sessions of uninterrupted meditation lasting for seven, twenty-one or forty-nine days, so do Pure Land devotees undertake intensive meditation for periods of that length. Often the meditation hall or recitation hall of a monastery is used. So stringent are the rules that, during a session, only three hours daily are spent in sleep! Allowing a total of from three to four hours for two short rituals, three simple meals, ablutions and rest periods, the time spent in formal recitation is from seventeen to eighteen hours a day; and, as talking is not permitted at meals or during the rest periods, it is likely that informal recitation takes up most of the time allotted for eating and rest. Thus invocation actually continues for around twenty hours daily. The effect of erasing extraneous thoughts for such long periods is highly beneficial. Vast accumulations of ego-centred thinking, petty cares and real anxieties are obliterated. Freed from this burden, the mind becomes clear and bright like a mirror from which mist and dust have been lovingly rubbed away. No wonder such sessions are effective in promoting realisation of reality's true face – Mind!

Chapter 8

Dreams, Reveries and Speculations

Imbued with supernatural power
And wise in using skilful means,
In every corner of the world
She manifests her countless forms.
Lotus Sūtra

Close on four decades have passed since the night of Kuan Yin's festival when I felt a sudden recognition of something loved and lost, a hint of memory stemming perhaps from a previous life. Nothing would be gained by my revisiting the sacred mountain, even if I had the opportunity. No longer do solemn sounds of mantric invocation and the wooden-fish drum's haunting notes reverberate upon the air, only the immemorial sigh of wind in the bamboos, the mournful cries of sea-birds winging inland from the Eastern Ocean and, perchance, the laughter of holiday-makers set free for the day from some neighbouring commune. What has come of my preoccupation with Kuan Yin Bodhisattva down the years? Needless to write of how much I have enjoyed the artistry with which her likeness is portrayed, whether painted on wall-scrolls or folding fans, incised on jade or ivory, carved in precious woods, moulded in bronze or fashioned in shining porcelain; were I to make much of this enthusiasm, Kuan Yin's laughter would ring out. 'Surely you know that a single small kindness is an offering more acceptable to me than a life-size statue carved by a master carver in flawless jade? Have you no more to say?'

I could argue that I have grown a little kinder with the years, but then that is true of so many people of my age and may well result from a waning of the fires of self-love for lack of fuel, from the lazy tolerance of a comfortably off old man who refuses to let things bother him. Or I could urge that Kuan Yin, in her Tara form, has been the vehicle of my yogic contemplations, that I have visualised light from her mentally created image flooding my being, that her mantra is often on my lips, but would she not reply: 'And so? In universes countless in number as Ganges sands there are gods and goddesses who have heard the voices of their devotees more often. Thus was it in your world with Isis, Artemis and Aphrodite; so is it now with that Mary who is worshipped in many climes as Queen of Heaven, so too with Kali who rejoices still in the blood of sacrificial victims, and many, many others.'

'True, Holy One, but I fancy their devotees demean them by insisting that the worshipped is exclusive of the worshippers and therefore less than infinite. I, Holy One, have learnt that you are infinite, that you and I are one and that, like every sentient being, I share your own divinity. I know well that the dualism which divides men from their gods is a delusion born of the drifting mists of primordial delusion.'

Would she not laugh at my making such a pompous affirmation while still so much afflicted by an illusory feeling of otherness towards all that lies outside my skin? 'Dear man, how you play with words! Your tongue, long and coiling as a sea-serpent, is forever there to trip you. Do you not find that tiresome?'

In an actual conversation with Kuan Yin, I should be sadly vanquished. Even supposing I have glimpsed, thanks to my teachers, a tiny facet of the truth, there are more pitfalls involved in putting it into words than holes in a fishing-net. Silence is best, silence and tranquillity of mind – a mind alert but as devoid of object as a lantern beam shining on untrodden snow. But then, if words are never to be used, would not one be guilty of hoarding knowledge like miser's gold? Though mystical truth is no sooner expressed than it vanishes like water poured on to parched sand, may not some of the drops be glimpsed while falling and encourage a quest for their original source?

The dialogue set forth above is purely imaginary, but there

have been others wherein the boundary between actual and imagined has been harder to define. Now and then a meditator falls into visionary dreams which, though guided at the start by his own whim, lead to strange and unforeseen conclusions. After all, if indeed the celestial Bodhisattvas are indivisible from mind, who is to say that thoughts seemingly voluntary are not from time to time inspired? Once I was led into a notable reverie by the following circumstance.

In Kanchanburi, a provincial town lying some distance to the east of the Thai–Burmese border, stands a small temple to Kuan Yin that I came upon for the first time just two years ago. While burning incense there, I noticed a Chinese gentleman and two ladies watching me with some amusement and heard the younger lady say: 'Well! Of the many strange things below heaven, a red-fur devil offering incense to Kuan Yin is not the least!' I am not, as it happens, a hairy man and the hair on my head is nearer black than red, but Southeast Asia-born Chinese habitually speak of Westerners as though, besides being devils, we were all of us covered with thick red hair like foxes!

Thinking to have a little fun, after rising from my knees, I made them a low bow and exclaimed pointedly, using a polite honorific for married women: 'T'ai-T'ai, have you not heard that Kuan Yin is no less gracious to animals and *devils* than to human-beings like yourself?'

This reproof, so unexpectedly delivered in their own tongue, produced satisfactory consternation; but they were pleasant people – an elderly couple and their niece recently arrived from Penang in Malaysia – and, to make amends for unintentional rudeness, they insisted on my dining with them at a nearby restaurant where they had arranged for special vegetarian food to be served to them throughout their brief stay. Over melon soup and some bowls of cooked lettuce garnished with mushrooms, beancurd, bamboo-shoots and 'tree-ear' fungus, Mrs Yeo, the younger lady, asked whether Kuan Yin sometimes sent me auspicious dreams. This was a reasonable question, for such dreams are among the recognised fruits of yogic meditation on a chosen being, but I gathered it was a prelude to some such experience of their own. And so it proved to be, for Mrs Lee, the aunt, now told me that she had been to Kanchanburi once before and, after visiting the temple where we had met, had had a peculiarly vivid dream.

She had found herself standing in a sea-side temple of palatial proportions, magnificently decorated with gilded wood-carving, pearl and coral ornaments and silken banners inscribed with invocations to Kuan Yin – a place ten thousand times more splendid than any she had seen in her travels. Its most extraordinary feature was a large and empty throne where the image should have been, a throne so perfectly resembling a prodigious lotus as to seem like a living flower with dew actually sparkling on its satiny petals! Soft music played on flute, dulcimer and bells was provided by invisible musicians and an unknown fragrance of surpassing sweetness filled the air. Prostrating herself before the throne, she rose to behold the thousand-armed Kuan Yin seated there in all her majesty, a great panoply of shining emblems in her thousand hands, a nimbus radiating from her body that was brighter than the sun yet softer on the eye than moonlight. Gazing sadly and not without severity at the kneeling lady, the Bodhisattva pronounced the following words in tones of unimaginable sweetness: 'When you were a baby still known as Ying-Ying, you suffered from a breathing sickness and your good mother vowed that, should you be allowed to live, you and she would abstain from the flesh of sentient beings throughout your lives. She kept this vow until the end, but you since your marriage have broken it daily for more than thirty years. Why so? That is not as it should be.'

While Mrs Lee, shaken and abashed was casting about for an answer, the dream had ended abruptly and she had awakened, face wet with tears. As it happened, all her immediate family were Buddhist and had been so impressed by the dream related on her return to Penang that her husband – the very man who had wooed her away from vegetarianism because of the social inconveniences – had been the first to suggest that they all stick to 'a pure diet' henceforth, and so they had. Now, believing that so unusual a dream might be connected with a peculiar quality of the image in that temple, she and her husband had brought their niece to worship there in the hope that all three of them would have inspiring dreams.

Much impressed by the story, I, too, hoped for an auspicious dream that night, but had none. As to the Lees and Mrs Yeo,

I cannot say, for I left the town before dawn and did not return until some days later. By then, enquiries about them were fruitless; at the temple, the only one of the old women caretakers who happened to be about knew nothing of the people I described and seemed mildly surprised to hear they had come all the way from Malaysia in the hope that the image she dusted every day would inspire dreams. However, returning to Bangkok that same afternoon and going into my Chinese garden to enjoy the cool hour before sunset, I did fall into a reverie so astonishingly vivid that I cannot help supposing there was something in what the Chinese family had surmised. I propose to describe the reverie as accurately as I can; but, to be perfectly frank, I cannot say to what extent its sequence was consciously induced by my own mind. It certainly seemed to happen of itself.

I was seated on one of those porcelain tubs which in Chinese gardens perform the function of chairs, their beauty being impervious to the weather, and happened to be facing a part of the rockery containing a small china figure of Kuan Yin half hidden by ferns and dwarf bamboos. Presently I fell into a state between sleeping and waking of a kind in which dreams may occur, though usually with a certain amount of conscious direction. After a little while, I seemed to be standing before Kuan Yin in a large cave which, on account of the sound of distant surf, I took to be the Hai Ch'ao Cave on P'u T'o Island, though it may well have been one of my own imagining. Except for my sensing that the figure seated on a rock in front of me radiated a tremendous and awesome power, she appeared more like a human than a goddess, being dressed in head-dress and robe of plain white cloth with no ornaments or emblems of any kind, nor anything like a nimbus, only a soft glow that made every detail of her person clearly visible against the darkness behind. Filled now with a delicious sense of well-being and exceedingly happy, I made to prostrate myself, but she motioned me back and sat watching my expression with a smile as though waiting for me to speak. Fearing to spend time on courteous preliminaries, lest she vanish before I had done, I blurted out the question that had occupied my mind on and off ever since our first encounter.

'Who and *what* are you, Holy One?'

Does it seem strange that, after all those years, I still needed to ask that question? *She* did not seem to think so, for instantly there came drifting into my mind the familiar Chinese proverb which runs: 'What can a well-frog know of the sky's immensity?', meaning in that context: 'Can a finite mind presume to grasp the infinite?' Of course not! Even as a child, I had felt some contempt for parsons and school-masters who spoke as though perfectly familiar with God's will, and had dismissed their impious nonsense as being of less account than the murmuring of bees. Now, emboldened by her winning smile, I continued: 'Holy One, I venture to suppose you are known, or at least dimly perceived, by many who have not as much as heard your name. Are you not the source of all wisdom from the first intimations of blissful Thusness to a Buddha's Complete Unexcelled Enlightenment? Are you not the mother of all deities? And, that being so, besides being one with all celestial Buddhas and Bodhisattvas, are you not also that which some call Brahma and others the Jade Emperor, Allah, Jahveh, God?'

Shocked by my own temerity, I watched lest her face grow stern. Had I inadvertently fallen into what Buddhists take to be the most dangerous of all errors – a dualism between worshipper and worshipped? Had I betrayed some lingering fragment of theistic thinking?

No! Her smile did not fade. She knew I had not demeaned her by confusing her with God or attributed to her the hideous cruelty of creating a world in which creatures live by devouring one another's flesh! Rather I had meant that the notion of God is born of a faint presentiment of Thusness, of which Kuan Yin herself and the other celestial Bodhisattvas are embodiments that spring forth from the depths of consciousness, perceptible to the inner eye and not distorted to fit in with the ancient Jewish conception of a creator God and one separate from his creatures. Thusness, being inconceivable to minds subject to normal human limitations, has to be contemplated in symbolic form; all the gods and goddesses in the universe are reflections of Mind, the container and contained, or vehicles of the beneficent forces proceeding from it. Seemingly my thought was acceptable. As though to illustrate the truth of divinity with innumerable aspects, the Bodhisattva startled me by manifesting herself in a veritable whirl of transformations, appearing now as Avalokita with eleven heads, now as the mirror-bearing, many-armed Chên-T'i, now as the horse-headed Hayagrīva, now as Tara, now as a terrifying wrathful-seeming deity not unlike Yamantaka, the blue, bull-headed Conqueror of Death, now as the handsome youth Manjusri – all of these alternating with many unnameable forms, male and female, horrendous and sublime, one merging into another like the changing patterns in a child's kaleidoscope! At the last, she appeared as No Thing, a vast, serene emptiness into which the cave and its surroundings presently dissolved. For a brief moment I felt terror; then the *skandhas* or constituents of my 'I-ness' burst into tiny fragments and were swept along into total annihilation! Recovering as from a long swoon, though possibly of less than a second's duration, I saw everything as before with Kuan Yin seated on her rock laughing melodiously. Then her figure became indistinct and was lost in the surrounding darkness, which gradually receded, giving place to twilight that quietly faded into night.

Fully awake and with scarcely time to feel the pangs of that tragic forlornness which follows such separations, I suddenly began exulting in the conviction of having just received a momentous revelation. My mind was bursting with the novelty of the thought: 'Beings should choose their own embodiments of divinity' and the words themselves seemed to thunder in my ears. 'Of course, of course!' I shouted (or so it seemed). 'It is not enough to reject the absurd conceptions foisted on us as children. They must be replaced with something able to pour forth inspiration glowing and sparkling like the magical elixir sought by Taoist sages, like the nectar of immortality that flows from Kuan Yin's vase! Since impenetrable mists preclude us from conceiving of Thusness as It Is, since our symbols are a billion billion yojanas from the reality depicted, we must at least seek worthy embodiments of its splendour. We must cease unctuously exposing children to boring sermons, to affirmations of belief in which we have little or no faith ourselves, to notions of vengeful deities befouled by the smoke of burnt offerings, to symbols of agonising death quite opposite to a child's inborn concept of what is good and beautiful and joyous. Children's innate perceptions must not be smothered but set free! Had this long ago been seen to, our modern world would not provide so many hideous instances of the consequences of discarding spiritual belief and spiritual endeavour. Our contemporaries would not be so ready to accept the coarse findings of their senses for reality itself! The mountains of evil wrought by this stultifying error which now rise on every hand would never have come into existence! Our children must be saved from tasting the bitter fruits of cynical unbelief. How?

'We must build upon their natural sense of awe and reverence, their belief in spirits, gods and fairies. We must tell them frankly that, since few can behold and none describe reality – a vast and glorious immensity immeasurably further than the furthest stars and nearer than the eyebrows to the eyes – they must choose for it symbols lovely, glowing, joyous as their minds can make them. How happy their response if, before "shades of the prison-house close in" upon their natural intuitions of all-pervading beauty, each child is encouraged to seek a symbolic form uniquely adorable to him, a form to become the object of his worship and the vehicle of mystical perception that transcends all symbols. The pursuit of spiritual perfection, no longer grudgingly accepted as a tiresome duty, will be filled with laughing zest. Filled with joyous awe, children will press forward with an enthusiasm that may carry them in the space of a single life-span to the glorious apotheosis of mystical endeavour – Enlightenment!'

I wonder if I have at all succeeded in capturing the exaltation that burnt into my mind as the tropic night closed swiftly down upon my garden, leaving rocks and plants but faintly illumined by lights shining from the windows which drew from the porcelain figure of Kuan Yin a soft and ghostly gleam? I went to bed later in the evening still intoxicated with that glorious revelation; but with the next day's dawning, after a heavy storm, came the deflation that so often follows in its turn. Longing to recapture something of my previous mood, I visited the rain-soaked garden in the early hours, only to find disconsolate bamboos and trees with dripping branches lowered as though in admonition. Dank sprays of bourgainvillæa let fall their sodden flowers and sighed. The sky prepared to shed more tears. To a lizard that paused to stare at me with cold hostility, I admitted having given way to gross presumption. How had I dared to dream of solving the ills of the world by advocating a return to what men of learning call 'primitive superstition'? Above all, how could I suppose that mothers and fathers would willingly allow children to choose their own gods?

Now, two years later, I am less sure that my mind was not truly inspired that evening. I remember how, on my first visit to the mountainous homeland of the Adamantine Vehicle of Buddhism, Vajrayana, one tip of which embraces the area round Gangtok, Kalimpong, Darjeeling, I had been struck by a phenomenon very close to the choosing of one's own embodiment of divinity. The choice placed before Tibetan neophytes ranges widely among hosts of divinities of every conceivable aspect – hideous or lovely, wrathful or benign. Of these, the one that calls forth special devotion is chosen as the *idam* thenceforth to become no mere symbol of divinity, but the actual yogic vehicle for coming face to face with Thusness! In those surroundings, by an irony of circumstance, I had gained a good part of such insight as I have into Kuan Yin's nature – not in China where she reigned in so many hearts, but among Tibetans to whom (except in her male aspect as Chenresigs or Avalokita, or else as Tara), she is unknown! But that is not to say I have ever come to a full understanding of her nature. Whether or not my own supposition, set forth in connection with my reverie, is accepted as the fruit of correct intuition, I can claim no warranty of its being fully endorsed by any Chinese monk or Tibetan lama. The pronouncements of my teachers have always been so ambivalent as to suggest no irreconcilable difference between conceiving of Kuan Yin as independently existing and as indivisible from the devotee's own mind. They would certainly go along with the Venerable Hsüan Hua's statement that, in paying homage to such beings, we are ultimately paying homage to ourselves; but taking that to mean that they do not exist independently in any sense would be to court a rebuke; yet so would a direct statement to the opposite effect, namely that they do have an independent existence of their own! By these mystically endowed men the two concepts are not deemed mutually exclusive; it is here that Western training with its insistence on irreconcilable logical categories forms an obstacle to understanding. The one way to reach the truth is to abandon discursive argument and approach it yogically, that is to say by cultivating direct perception.

An anecdote from my last days in Peking (1948) illustrates the problem well. I had gone to take a farewell look at Pai T'a Szû, a Mongol temple with a very fine *chorten* (reliquary tower) which I had not visited since before the war. Once teeming with lamas, it now wore a deserted look; the few lamas still in residence looked seedy and neglected; but they welcomed me hospitably with tea and slightly sweetened dough-cakes fried in oil. These were served on a low table around which we sat cross-legged on a brick sleeping-platform covered with fine but woefully dilapidated carpets. Our conversation veered to their favourite Bodhisattva, Avalokita, whereat the senior lama related a tale about his teacher, a Pao-T'ou youth who, at the age of twelve, had followed his own teacher to Urga where they lived in a temple that was really a fenced enclosure dotted with *yurts* (felt tents) from the midst of which rose a brick prayer-hall built around a statue of the Bodhisattva in his eleven-headed aspect – He-Who-Sees-In-All-Directions. Speaking Chinese in the flat toneless Mongol manner and using the Chinese name, Kuan Yin, for the Bodhisattva, the old man, having described something of his teacher's childhood days, continued:

'Once it chanced that, having displeased his lama by some carelessness or other, he was commanded to pass an entire night making grand prostrations before Kuan Yin's statue – not the ordinary kind but throwing himself repeatedly at full length on the floor. Need I say it was exhausting for a child? Towards midnight he desisted and sat warily upon a cushion, ready to spring up at the first intimation of someone's approach. The altar lamps cast fitful shadows and, as there was no knowing what might be lurking in the surrounding darkness, he became afraid and started gabbling Kuan Yin's mantra. Presently in the corner housing the shrine of the guardian deities, he saw three pairs of fiery eyes and, though he tried to believe they were no more than the jewelled eyes of images caught by the light streaming from the altar, he grew fearful lest the guardians were about to spring out and punish his impiety in resting from his prostrations. Well drilled in monastic discipline, he would sooner risk being devoured by the terrible guardians than leave the prayer-hall without his lama's permission; he had to bear his terror, teeth chattering so loudly that he seemed to hear the rattle of bones. At last, recollecting what he had been taught of such matters, he ceased his gabble and, concentrating with all his might, uttered Kuan Yin's mantra just once from his heart as loudly as he dared – OMMMMMMMMM MANI PADME HŪMMMMMMMMMMMMMMM!!!

'Instantly a living replica of the gilded image, alike in all respects except that it was smaller and had the colour of pure gold, glided from behind the altar and, touching him upon the crown, sent waves of bliss flowing downwards to the extremities of his body that caused trunk and limbs to tingle with delight.

'In the hour before dawn, the noises made by people stirring in the kitchen woke him from a dreamless sleep while he was actually in the act of making a grand prostration and he recollected that he had been performing them all through the night! Yet even now his movements were as effortless as those of a wrestler newly risen from a night's rest!'

As this story drew to its climax, the old monk watched my face with innocent delight, never dreaming that there might be people in the world more likely to disbelieve than be edified by this artless tale of the Bodhisattva's compassion. Phrasing my question cautiously, I enquired whether the golden image would have been seen by anyone who had happened to enter the prayer-hall at that time.

'Assuredly!' he answered in surprise. 'Our Bodhisattva would not deny that felicity even to a thieving Kirgiz nomad, a worshipper of the god A-La (Allah).'

'So the image was not born from your teacher's own mind?'

Puzzled, the old man cast me a reproachful look as though beginning to wonder whether, on account of his patched and ragged garb, I could have so little respect for him as to suppose him a liar. 'Your words are strange. Does not Kuan Yin always exist in *and* outside people's minds?'

Eagerly I assented and harmony was restored, but inwardly I marvelled to note that he was unable to perceive an incongruity that must be immediately obvious to a Westerner's mind. To most of us it would seem that either an occurrence is mind-born and, if so, visible only to its creator; or else it is materially real and therefore visible to all. Since then, of course, I have learnt not to be so sure that the two possibilities are mutually exclusive.

Such stories cannot be dismissed as fabrications, for they are often told by men who would scorn to lie. To Kuan Yin's devotees these things happen and, whether they occur as material manifestations that could be photographed or as psychological experiences that only seem to belong to external reality, they are equally miracles. Very recently I chanced upon a clear example of a third mode of being, neither wholly internal nor entirely external. A visiting lama from Nepal, an Englishman by birth, told me last month of an incident that occurred when, one night during a visit to England to see his mother, he happened to share a bedroom with a boy in his early teens. So as not to draw unnecessary attention to himself, he performed his evening yoga mentally and then composed himself for sleep. In the morning the boy declared that, waking several times, he had noticed with amazement a covering of light over his roommate's bed and that, when at about midnight the lama had got up to relieve himself in the bathroom, the light had followed and returned with him. Now this boy, though obviously a child with unusual psychic powers, knew nothing of Buddhism and had no idea that a lama, before going to sleep, invokes his *idam* and creates in his mind a 'vajra-tent', a protective covering that is held to remain in place until morning. The fact that the boy, who had never heard of any such thing, perceived the vajra-tent, or at least its radiance, suggests that what is yogically visualised manifests itself in a way that is neither wholly confined to the adept's own mind, nor so solidly material as to be visible to everybody. I believe the key to many mysteries is to be found here.

This incident may *indirectly* throw a little light upon the manner in which monks and lamas conceive of a celestial Bodhisattva's nature. No knowledgeable Buddhist supposes they exist precisely in the sense that this printed page exists or in the sense that Aphrodite was believed to exist as a divine inhabitant of Mount Olympus; but there is plenty of evidence to support a conviction that there are modes of existence too subtle to be classed with that of physical objects, yet too clearly perceptible to the senses of psychically gifted or yogically trained third parties to be dismissed as pure imagination. I do *not* mean that the nature of the lama's vajra-tent provides a close analogy to the nature of Kuan Yin, for I deem the tent to be but one of a wide and progressively subtle range of entities lying between the fully material and wholly psychic categories. The purpose of relating the anecdote was merely to illustrate that there are several modes of being.

I hesitate to go further. There are matters too sublime to be set down unless in the light of certain knowledge. Not being a man of much attainment, I have no head for awesome heights. To write in ignorance may do harm. Should one wish to go on from here, books will not do. The way is to practise a yoga leading to direct perception. For this, however, there are certain prerequisites. The adept must live frugally and chastely lest he squander his energy; and he must act selflessly, compassionately and with perfect impartiality towards all sentient beings. Moreover, entrance to the yogic path can scarcely be made without a teacher; but some account of its earlier stages may be of interest. That one should take Kuan Yin or Tara as the vehicle is by no means essential, but it is traditionally taught that these two beings are easier to woo than some others, such as the shy Manjusri, embodiment of wisdom.

Stage 1. At the outset, it is necessary to woo the *idam* or indwelling deity as though he (she) were an external divinity, even though one may know that this is not so. Pure offerings, such as incense, flowers and water, must be made, but never the flesh of sentient beings. By the power of visualisation supported by mantras, the water is converted into treasures – namely all that one has of body, speech and mind, all good qualities and properties, all merits, as well as all imaginable precious things including the universe itself, ornamented with sun and moon. It is yogically desirable at this stage that the *idam* be viewed as though he (she) really valued the kind of offerings one makes to kings, though most of them are in fact mentally created. (One of the purposes may be to provide a response to man's primitive but deep-seated belief in deities external to the worshipper, deities who make royal demands, like Artemis who required the blood of pigeons, or Jehovah who rejoiced in burnt offerings and demanded the suffering and death of his son as the price of human redemption. Perhaps early Buddhist teachers found it advisable to accept the traditional practices of new converts and transmute them by stages into purer forms. Perhaps human psychology still requires a quasi-theistic approach at the beginning. I do not know. It is always best to follow the instructions of one's yogically advanced teachers.)

Stage 2. The *idam* is invited to pass from a mentally created image into the adept's body for a space, that the perfect union of worshipper and worshipped may be accomplished in a manner that leads naturally from stage 1. (At this point, the adept may still be unaware from direct experience – though he will surely know it theoretically – that *idam* and worshipper have never been apart.)

Stage 3. The *idam*, having again been invited, is retained in the adept's body for as long as he feels able to conduct himself consonantly with his exalted role as a Bodhisattva, free from the least hint of self-centred thought or action. (The period of union is gradually increased and the determined adept may elect to spend up to seven years in solitary seclusion, the better to perfect the divine qualities of compassion, equanimity, egolessness and so forth.)

Stage 4. The union remains permanent and gives birth to direct mystical perception of the identity of self and other, of the realm of form and the Great Void. Wisdom and compassion are united and the path to Enlightenment immeasurably shortened.

Among readers of this final chapter, there will be none, I hope, who doubt my sincerity. All are welcome to suppose me the victim of errors and delusions resulting from the inexpert use of yogic knowledge; and who is to say they would not be justified? If, however, there are any who have followed me thus far and who accept what I have written as being reasonable, I owe them an apology. Having offered glimpses of the Bodhisattva Kuan Yin at many levels, starting with her as a goddess of fisher-folk, I have broken off leaving her a shadowy figure to the end. I am sorry for that, but what can I do? I must not *invent* a climax to the quest. There is really no way to go further, short of undertaking the appropriate yoga right up to its final stage and achieving direct intuitive perception. To those who do this successfully, her secret will most surely be revealed.

One thing is certain – though pursuit of the Bodhisattva may at first be motivated by an idle whim, if carried through it leads to exalted heights of mystical experience. Whole universes become playthings of the adept's mind. Together with the indescribable joy of increasing identification with the Bodhisattva comes perception of the identity of self and other. Insignificant foot-hills are succeeded by cloud-wrapped peaks and the path, becoming ever steeper and more hazardous, leads thence to expanses of pure white snow awful to contemplate until presently lit by a roseate glow. The glow becomes a shining light, the shining light a blaze of sudden understanding, and then?

Beyond that lies a state transcending the furthest confines of conceptual thought. Now does the Compassionate Bodhisattva terrify, being at last revealed as one with an immensity too vast for finite beings to contemplate. The cowering ego shrieks and, fighting for its very being, rends mind and body with agonising pains. 'Back, back!' it wails. 'Before us looms insanity, an ocean of inconceivable horror wherein we shall disintegrate! Here lies the end, a boundless nothingness, an unspeakably fearful and hideous void wherein we shall be shattered, dissolved, annihilated! Aieeeeeeeeeeeeeeh!'

Ere long the ego is no more. Caught by rays of the Clear Light of Reality, it shrivels, shrinks and is utterly consumed. Now is the Bodhisattva fully revealed. Her erstwhile devotee, by no means annihilated, has undergone an infinite expansion and contains within what he had once deludedly mistaken for 'himself' a myriad myriad universes, a Thusness so vast and comprehensive that not one grain of 'otherness' remains. Henceforth an eternity of bliss, the unutterable bliss of Nirvāna – final liberation – supervenes!

The Principal Iconographic Forms of the Bodhisattva

As Kuan Yin

In China, Japan and neighbouring countries, female depictions of Kuan Yin predominate, generally in idealised human form with one head and two arms. Her long robe and characteristic hood-like head-dress may be white or coloured. The splendid ornaments sometimes adorning head, throat, wrists and ankles are a conventional symbol of her Bodhisattvahood, but these are often lacking so as to achieve a chaste nun-like effect. Some depictions are devoid of clearly defined sexual attributes and occasionally she is shown in male form; for instance, in very old paintings or those in ancient style, the face may be lightly bearded. The commonest male forms reveal the full splendour of a Bodhisattva, the garments and ornaments being similar to those of ancient Hindu rulers.

When the figure is depicted standing, the feet may rest upon a giant lotus petal that is perhaps floating upon the sea, or on the calyx of a huge lotus bloom, for this flower is especially associated with the embodiments of compassion – Amitābha Buddha, Avalokita, Tara and Kuan Yin – though, as one of the most widespread of Buddhist symbols, it may also appear among the emblems of many other Buddhist deities. Kuan Yin's body when standing is often gracefully curved with one shoulder held a little higher than the other, the head slightly inclined and the hands hidden by long sleeves, unless she stands with one hand raised, the other pointing downwards in the attitude of benediction.

When she is depicted sitting down, both feet may be placed on the ground, or the right leg may rest on the left thigh or else be raised so that the foot rests upon whatever she is sitting on, or the right foot may be slightly extended, Tara fashion, as though she is about to rise from meditation.

Sometimes she is seen alone, sometimes attended by Shan Ts'ai, a handsome youth or child, and by Lung Nü, the Dragon Maiden, holding out a giant pearl. Or she may appear to the right of a trinity known as the Three Holy Ones, with Amitābha Buddha in the centre and Mahāsthāmaprapta (Ta Shih Chih) Bodhisattva symbolising perfect activity to the left.

Her principal emblems are a precious vase held in one hand and a willow spray held in the other, symbolising respectively 'sweet dew' (also known as *amṙta*) meaning the nectar of wisdom and compassion, and secondly her willingness to sprinkle it upon the heads of all who invoke her aid.

A child seated on her lap or a group of children playing about her symbolises her ability to bestow children of the desired sex endowed with many perfections of mind and body.

A seascape or running water in the background suggest her sea-girt paradise, Potala or Potalaka Mountain.

As the Chên-T'i Kuan Shih Yin, she has eighteen arms, and mirrors are much in evidence.

As the Holy One, she stands with one arm raised in benediction.

As the Bestower of the Wish-Fulfilling Gem, she sits upon a lotus throne, one foot raised, four arms, cheek resting on her hand.

As Willow Kuan Yin, she sits beneath a willow tree, a spray of willow in her right hand, her left hand held to the chest palm outwards in Tara fashion.

As a vehicle for contemplative yoga, she resembles the white, one-headed, four-armed Avalokiteśvara (q.v.). Similarly, in almost any of her multi-headed, multi-armed forms, she is barely if at all distinguishable from the Bodhisattva, who is, as it were, her other self. This is the case with the thousand-eyed thousand-armed Kuan Yin, whether with one head or eleven.

There are many other less common forms, of which two of the most interesting are Kuan Yin riding upon clouds with bow, arrows and shield in her hands to make war upon evil (never upon unfortunate evil-doers, however); and Kuan Yin depicted almost exactly like a Buddha-figure seated in meditation, but with a truly enormous beard! Moreover, she is identified with the three-headed Hayagrīva under the name Ma T'ou (Horse-Headed) Kuan Yin.

In just one context (and only in Japan), Kuan Yin is actually given the title *Buddha*; by some strange chance, she has come to be numbered among the thirteen Buddhas invoked by Shingon devotees during obsequies for the dead.

Kuan Yin's principal emblems

The following list has been taken from a Chinese edition of the Heart of Dhāranī of Great Compassion Sūtra:

1 The Wish Fulfilling Gem, signifying attainment of all wholesome wishes.
2 A rope, wherewith she binds all harmful circumstances.
3 A jewelled bowl, containing cures for maladies.
4 A sword, for subduing water spirits.
5 A vajra or two-headed adamantine sceptre, sometimes wrongly called a thunder-bolt, for subduing demons.
6 A vajra-dagger, for bringing about the capitulation of enemies.
7 One hand held out with fingers and thumb pointing upwards so that it somewhat resembles a bowl, for subduing fear.
8 A solar disc containing a bird, for banishing darkness.
9 A lunar disc containing a rabbit, for counteracting poison.
10 A bow, signifying a glorious career.
11 An arrow, to bring friends nigh.
12 A willow branch, for driving away sickness.
13 A white brush or flag-shaped duster, for banishing hardships.
14 A 'long-life' vase, signifying all that is virtuous and loving.
15 A dragon-headed tablet, for subduing wild beasts.
16 An axe, signifying protection against oppressive authorities.
17 A jade bracelet (somewhat rounded and yet roughly triangular), to obtain filial service from sons and daughters.
18 A white lotus, signifying the attainment of merit.
19 A blue lotus, signifying rebirth in a Pure Land.
20 A precious mirror, signifying *prajñā*, wisdom.

21 A purple lotus, signifying that one will behold the Bodhisattvas.

22 A jewelled bowl of fruit, for escaping from pits.

23 A cloud of five colours, for entering upon the way of the immortals.

24 A water-bottle resting on the palm, for rebirth in a Brahma-loka (nebulous heaven).

25 A red lotus, for attaining rebirth in a *deva-loka* (a heaven less abstract than a *Brahma-loka*).

26 A halberd, for counteracting the effects of people's dishonesty.

27 A conch-shell, for summoning *devas* (gods) and beneficent spirits.

28 A club, to win command of spirits.

29 A rosary, wherewith to call upon the Buddhas of the Ten Quarters to come swiftly to one's succour (i.e. to welcome one to a Pure Land).

30 A vajra-topped bell, wherewith to achieve marvellous musical accomplishments.

31 A precious seal, wherewith to obtain the gift of eloquence.

32 A hook, wherewith to command the protection of benevolent *devas* and dragon-kings.

33 A monk's iron-tipped staff, signifying a compassionate desire to protect others.

34 Two hands palm to palm but not quite touching, signifying capacity to revere and love all sentient beings.

35 A Buddha figure surrounded by a nimbus and seated on a lotus, signifying spending life after life with the Buddhas always at one's side.

36 A palatial pavilion, signifying that one dwells life after life in the palace of the Buddhas.

37 A precious volume, wherewith to achieve great learning.

38 A golden wheel, signifying that from this very life until the attainment of Buddhahood, the Wheel of Enlightenment will never cease to turn for us.

39 Two hands wrist to wrist with the fingers nearly horizontal and pointing to right and left, and with a Buddha figure floating just above, for summoning the Buddhas of the Ten Quarters to bestow empowerment and to predict certain success in attaining Enlightenment.

40 A bunch of grapes, for ensuring bountiful harvests of fruit and crops.

41 The hand held open, fingers pointing downwards with the nectar of wisdom and compassion (known as sweet dew) pouring from the eye in the centre of the palm, wherewith to assuage hunger and thirst.

42 Right hand resting on the left, palms upward, signifying power to subjugate vengeful spirits in all the innumerable universes.

Finely wrought statues or paintings of Kuan Yin may depict her forty-two principal hands holding these emblems or forming these mudras. The initiate may use the emblems and mudras, each with its appropriate mantra, to attain the ends they signify.

As Avalokiteśvara (Avalokita)

In Tibet, Mongolia, Nepal and parts of Siberia where Avalokita is deeply revered, his aspects are invariably male; Kuan Yin is unknown, female attributes being ascribed only to his emanation, Tara. However, he shares with Kuan Yin the eleven-headed (and also the single-headed) thousand-eyed thousand-armed forms, the heads being arranged in three ascending tiers of three surmounted by two single heads, one above the other, of which the topmost is a Buddha-head signifying that he is an emanation of Amitābha Buddha. This multi-headed multi-armed form is sometimes known as Ekādaśamuka – The-One-Who-Looks-In-All-Directions. Like Kuan Yin, he is also identified with Hayagrīva, the so-called Horse-Headed.

For the purposes of contemplative yoga, he is visualised as possessing one head and four arms. In this form, he is white in colour and seated in the lotus posture; two of the arms are extended horizontally from the shoulders as far as the elbow, the forearms rising vertically and the right hand clasping a rosary, the left a lotus stem; the other pair of hands meet palm to palm at his breast in the attitude of prayer. This is the yogic aspect to which the mantra OM MANI PADME HŪM pertains.

When Avalokita appears as one of a trinity of Bodhisattvas,

he is usually flanked by Manjusri (embodiment of wisdom) and Vajrapani (embodiment of power), but in another trinity he and Manjusri are accompanied by Maitreya Bodhisattva who is destined to become the Buddha of the next aeon.

In his Padmapani (Lotus Bearer) aspect, he appears as a charming youth bearing a lotus. Other divinities with whom he is held to be more or less identical are Simhananda (the Lion-Voiced Lord), Vagaīsvara (Promulgator of the Eternal) and Lokeśvara, the aspect he wears chiefly in such countries as Cambodia and the former Champa in Southeast Asia. There are others.

As with Kuan Yin, multiple eyes signify power to see all sufferings in the universe simultaneously, multiple arms symbolise infinite power to succour, and a Buddha-head at the apex of his many heads indicates that he is an emanation of Amitābha Buddha or of the supreme wisdom-energy, Bodhi.

As Tara

A full description of Tara's appearance is given on pages 53 and 54.

As Miao Shan

The Chinese nun-princess, Miao Shan, has no special characteristics or emblems that are known to me, unless the white bird into which she was transmuted that she might escape from her burning prison. She is generally depicted in the long robes of a royal princess, or in a shorter robe that exposes some part of her wide silk trousers, and with high-piled hair elaborately arranged. Unfortunately so many Chinese ladies of antiquity closely resemble her in these particulars that it is difficult to identify her for certain, unless by the calligraphic inscription or by representations of one or more incidents from the Miao Shan legends forming part of the background.

Nomenclature

The Bodhisattva's most widely used Chinese names are Kuan Yin, Kuan Shih Yin and Kuan Tzû Tsai, of which the Cantonese variants are Kwoon Yam, Kwoon Sai Yam and Kwoon Chi Choi. In Viet-Nam her name is pronounced Quan Am. In Japan, she is generally known as Kwannon Bosatzu or Kwannon Sama, the former suffix being the Japanese rendering of Bodhisattva, whereas the latter is an honorific.

The Tibetan name for Avalokita is Chenresigs.

Glossary

Only foreign words sometimes unclear from the context are given. All are Sanskrit except those marked C (for Chinese), J (for Japanese) or T (for Tibetan).

Asura	A titan at war with heaven.
Bīja-mantra	Syllable containing a deity's essence.
Bod (T)	Tibet.
Bodhi	The urge to wisdom, compassion and Enlightenment.
Brahma	Supreme Hindu deity.
Chang (T)	Tibetan beer.
Deva	A general word for deities.
Dhāranī	(see Mantra)
Hsiu-ts'ai (C)	Civil service examination degree.
Kowtow (C)	To prostrate or a prostration.
Lama (T)	A monk or layman learned in religion.
Li (C)	Third of a mile.
Lo-fu (C)	Muleteer.
Mahayana	Northern or Greater Vehicle Buddhism.
Mantra	A group of sacred syllables of great power.
Mou (C)	Land measure, less than an acre.
Mudra	Sacred hand gesture.
Naga	Serpent-like being with some human characteristics.
Nirmānakāya	Body of Transformation, one of the three metaphysical bodies of a Buddha.
Nirvāna	Ultimate blissful state of being beyond 'I' and 'other'.
P'ei! (C)	An expression of scorn.
Prajñā	Transcendental Wisdom.
Preta	Tantalised ghost.
Sadhana	Contemplative rite involving visualisation.

Sama (J)	Title of respect.
Samādhi˙	State of objectless awareness.
Sambhogakāya	Body of Bliss, one of the three metaphysical bodies of a Buddha.
Saṃsara	The round of alternating birth and death not terminated until Enlightenment is attained.
Skandha	One of the five 'heaps' into which the illusory ego can be broken down.
Sūtra	A sacred text proclaimed by the Buddha himself.
T'ai T'ai (C)	A title similar to Madam or Mrs.
Tathāgata	'Thus Come', a title of the Buddha.
Theravada	Southern or Lesser Vehicle Buddhism.
Tripitaka	The sacred canon of Mahayana Buddhism.
Vajra	A sceptre-like symbol of Reality's adamantine nature.
Vajrayana	The tantric form of Buddhism practised in Tibet.
Yojana	A measure of length, thought to be equivalent to a day's march.

ALSO IN SHAMBHALA DRAGON EDITIONS

The Art of War, by Sun Tzu. Translated by Thomas Cleary.

Buddha in the Palm of Your Hand, by Osel Tendzin. Foreword by Chögyam Trungpa.

The Buddhist I Ching, by Chih-hsu Ou-i. Translated by Thomas Cleary.

Cutting Through Spiritual Materialism, by Chögyam Trungpa.

Dakini Teachings: Padmasambhava's Oral Instructions to Lady Tsogyal, by Padmasambhava. Translated by Erik Pema Kunsang.

The Dawn of Tantra, by Herbert V. Guenther & Chögyam Trungpa.

The Diamond Sutra and The Sutra of Hui-neng. Translated by A. F. Price and Wong Mou-lam. Forewords by W. Y. Evans-Wentz and Christmas Humphreys.

The Experience of Insight: A Simple and Direct Guide to Buddhist Meditation, by Joseph Goldstein.

Glimpses of Abhidharma, by Chögyam Trungpa.

The Heart of Awareness: A Translation of the Ashtavakra Gita. Translated by Thomas Byrom.

The Hundred Thousand Songs of Milarepa. Volumes 1 & 2. Translated by Garma C. C. Chang.

I Ching: The Tao of Organization, by Cheng Yi. Translated by Thomas Cleary.

I Ching Mandalas: A Program of Study for The Book of Changes. Translated & edited by Thomas Cleary.

Mastering the Art of War, by Zhuge Liang & Liu Ji. Translated & edited by Thomas Cleary.

The Myth of Freedom, by Chögyam Trungpa.

Nine-Headed Dragon River, by Peter Matthiessen.

Returning to Silence: Zen Practice in Daily Life, by Dainin Katagiri. Foreword by Robert Thurman.

Seeking the Heart of Wisdom: The Path of Insight Meditation, by Joseph Goldstein & Jack Kornfield. Foreword by H. H. the Dalai Lama.

Shambhala: The Sacred Path of the Warrior, by Chögyam Trungpa.

The Spiritual Teaching of Ramana Maharshi, by Ramana Maharshi. Foreword by C. G. Jung.

The Tantric Mysticism of Tibet, by John Blofeld.

The Tao of Politics: Lessons of the Masters of Huainan. Translated & edited by Thomas Cleary.

Tao Teh Ching, by Lao Tzu. Translated by John C. H. Wu.

The Tibetan Book of the Dead: The Great Liberation through Hearing in the Bardo. Translated with commentary by Francesca Fremantle & Chögyam Trungpa.

The Vimalakirti Nirdesa Sutra. Translated & edited by Charles Luk. Foreword by Taizan Maezumi Roshi.

The Way of the White Clouds: A Buddhist Pilgrim in Tibet, by Lama Anagarika Govinda. Foreword by Peter Matthiessen.

The Wheel of Life: The Autobiography of a Western Buddhist, by John Blofeld. Foreword by Huston Smith.

Zen Essence: The Science of Freedom. Translated & edited by Thomas Cleary.